A PARENT'S SURVIVAL GUIDE TO STARTING SECONDARY SCHOOL

Ease the transition for you and your child!

MOLLY POTTER

Published 2011 by A&C Black Publishers Limited
36 Soho Square, London W1D 3QY
www.acblack.com

ISBN 978-1-4081-313-98

Text © Molly Potter 2011
Design © Lynda Murray 2011
Illustrations © Antonio Papaleo 2011
Photographs © Fotolia

A CIP record for this publication is available from the British Library.

Printed in Great Britain by Latimer Trend & Company Ltd.

This book is produced using paper that is made from wood grown in
managed, sustainable forests. It is natural, renewable and recyclable.
The logging and manufacturing processes conform to the environmental
regulations of the country of origin.

To see our full range of titles visit **www.acblack.com**

Contents

Introduction

'The key to change... is to let go of fear' *Roseanne Cash*

It probably feels like only yesterday that your child was a baby and yet here they are ready to go to secondary school. How did that happen? It may seem too soon and bring out strong feelings of protectiveness and anxiety, but don't worry! Help is at hand – this book will show you and your child how to prepare for the exciting new experiences ahead.

How to use this book

This book is organised into chapters that follow the logical sequence from choosing a school to getting settled in. The final chapter provides invaluable information and advice on how to navigate through the difficult pre-teenage years:

→ Introduction

→ Choosing the 'right' school

→ Preparing for the move

→ Starting secondary school

→ Settling in

→ Heading for the teenage years.

The book provides the background information that will help you, as a parent/carer to anticipate any difficulties your child might experience with their move to secondary school. It is also full of advice, ideas and guidance for supporting your child through the process.

You can read the book from cover to cover or dip into relevant sections as you wish.

Supporting your child

Your role is really important in helping your child to feel comfortable and supported as they leave their primary school.

For your child, the move to secondary school causes a lot of change to adjust to in a relatively short amount of time. On top of these changes, many children are also starting puberty. This can mean they will want more independence, will be taking more notice of their peers and may be trying to redefine relationships with the adults in their lives.

If you think back to your own experiences, you will realise how useful it would have been (or was – if you were lucky enough to have one) to have a trusted adult to talk things through with.

A lot of your child's anxieties will be caused by exaggerated rumours and/or anticipation of some changes being harder to deal with than they really are. A key part of your support is helping your child to put the changes they're going to experience into perspective.

It's about helping them to realise that their worries might be:

*   worse in anticipation than reality

*   helped by being shared

*   actually something to look forward to if thought about in a different way.

You can be ready with useful advice about how to approach worries, however small, so they don't become big difficulties.

This book provides you with information, ideas, suggestions and guidance to help you adopt a supportive role in this potentially tricky stage of your child's life.

What might your child be worrying about?

The following comments were collected from children who were in their last term of primary school. While your child might not be anxious about all of the things here, it does show the type of worries they might have:

> We'll go from being the biggest in the school to being the babies.

- I think having a lot of different teachers will take some getting used to.
- I've heard that some of the teachers are really strict and all the children are scared of them.

> I'm worried about getting lost in such a big school.

- I've been told the big kids bully the new ones.
- We'll have to get used to new school rules and routines – and they have different punishments!
- I'll have to get up much earlier and walk further to get to my new school.

> I'll have to be more organised.

- You get loads more homework and the teachers are really strict about handing it in on time.
- The school grounds are so much bigger – break times will be quite different.
- Some of my best friends aren't going to the same secondary school as me. I feel really sad about this.
- I've got to catch a bus to school now. I used to walk.

- The work will get a lot harder.
- You have to take notes and write essays a lot. We haven't done much of that at primary school.
- Secondary school is all 'teenage' and all about needing to be cool. I worry that I won't fit in.
- I don't know what school lunch times will be like. I won't know what to choose for lunch.
- I'll miss primary school. I've been here for ages.
- I hope people talk to me so I can make new friends.

> I don't know where you store your stuff because you move classes all the time. Will I have to take my bag everywhere with me?

What might your child be looking forward to?

But it's not all negative. It is also easy to find things that children look forward to:

There will be new subjects and opportunities.

✓ I've heard there are more clubs to join.

✓ There is much more sports equipment and you can try things like trampolining.

✓ I'm looking forward to being treated in a more grown up way.

The school trips are more exciting.

✓ My older sister is at secondary school and she says it's great.

I'm quite excited by the whole idea.

✓ There will be people from different schools and lots of new friends to make.

✓ If you don't like one teacher, you're not stuck with them all the time!

✓ I bet after a couple of weeks it's like you've always been there.

✓ You get to use Bunsen burners!

How do schools help with transition?

In 2002 Ofsted (the body that carries out school inspections) flagged up that supporting pupils with the move (or 'transition') to secondary school was a long-standing weakness of our education system. Since then most schools have made efforts to address this.

Research published in 'What makes a successful transition from primary to secondary school' (DCSF 2008) suggests that a successful transition is when a child:

- ✓ develops new friendships and improves their self-esteem and confidence

- ✓ settles in so well to school life that they cause no concerns to their parents

- ✓ increases their interest in school and school work

- ✓ gets used to school routines and school organisation with great ease

- ✓ continues with a similar curriculum.

You will be able to find out what your child's primary and secondary school are doing to support the transition process (see page 9).

Secondary schools may be very good at helping children to get used to their new school's routines and procedures, become acquainted with staff, find their way round their new school building and make friends. However they may pay less attention to helping pupils adjust to having new lessons and new ways of teaching and learning.

What schools usually do

There are lots of things that schools can do to help new children settle in. Here are some examples:

Before the move

★ Open days where children experience lessons, look at examples of work and meet children who will be joining them from other primary schools.

★ Leaflets and booklets full of information about school procedures and what to expect.

★ Pupils in their first year of secondary school return to their primary school to talk to the children about what to expect and to answer questions.

★ Parents/carers evenings where the headteacher talks about the school and answers any questions.

★ Head of year visits to all the transition primary schools – to introduce themselves to the children so they are familiar with at least one face at secondary school.

Settling in after the move

★ Induction days before the existing pupils return for the beginning of term, so that new pupils can find their feet in their new school.

★ Team-building activities to help pupils make new friends.

★ A mentoring scheme – where older, existing pupils are allocated a new pupil to look out for.

★ Rules are relaxed when pupils first arrive – until they become used to them.

★ Form tutors run sessions that explore how pupils have adjusted to secondary school.

Helping the progress in learning

★ Secondary teachers visit the primary school in lesson time to consider children's talents, learning styles and the teaching styles they are used to.

★ Workbooks and/or exercise books that are used in primary school continue to be used for the first year at secondary school to provide some continuity. Using exercise books that transfer with the pupils to secondary school tends to raise children's effort in the last stage of primary school. It also gives their

new teachers a good indication of their capabilities so any dip in standards can be addressed.

★ Extra help is provided for school work and homework while pupils adjust to the new styles of teaching and learning.

★ Form tutors explore lessons pupils are struggling with and those they find interesting.

Choosing the 'right' school

At some point in your child's final year of primary school – often in the first term – you will receive notification from your local authority that you need to decide which secondary school you would like your child to go to. There may not be many options because of where you live but where there is a choice, you will probably want to consider this carefully.

Things to think about

Here is some general advice about selecting your child's secondary school:

Don't always believe a school's reputation.

Schools change all the time – especially if they undergo a change in leadership. A school's reputation can often be out of date or inaccurate in the first place!

A school's reputation can sometimes be an exaggerated response to a one-off mishap or poor management of one parent's perspective of a situation. Once a school gets a negative reputation, it can be quite hard to shake off – even if they have taken effective measures to address any concerns.

Some schools can also have a hard time with the local media – newspapers in particular. Remember that the media tends to look for a 'juicy' angle and that they are not always concerned about presenting every side of a story. For example, a school could gain a reputation for having a really bad bullying problem based on a news report sourced from one parent's viewpoint. The paper is happy to run the story because it is shocking

and newsworthy but may not represent the school's angle sufficiently well. So try not to form an opinion about a school based on a single newspaper report.

If you have worries based on a school's reputation, be prepared to ask questions at any parents' session that the school runs. The chances are your mind will be put at rest.

Terrible, awful, nasty bullying school!

Try asking your child:

? What have you heard about that particular school?

? Which friends would you most like to be at secondary school with?

? What do you think you will make you happy at secondary school?

? What do you think will be the most important thing you do at secondary school?

? What do you think I (the parent) believe is most important about secondary school?

Many parents trust their child to make the decision that will make them happy.

Consider your child's viewpoint

You might disagree with your child about the choice of school. It's important to listen to the reasons why your child wants to go a particular school. It might be that most of their friends are going to one school and if your child is very sociable, this will be extremely important to them. Try not to be flippant about this.

Your child might not want to go to a particular school because they've heard something about it which is causing them concern. Or your child might think that the school they want to go to has good points that you haven't considered. These might be features that you think are insignificant (such as the choice of food in the canteen, a particular school trip and so on).

The best thing you can do is start talking to your child about their preferences. The most effective way to influence your child's decision, if you feel you need to, is to find out more information about the schools in question.

11

All schools are different

The National Curriculum is statutory for all state schools and therefore curriculum content is pretty similar. Schools do, however, all have their own character. They differ in ways that are not necessarily to do with curriculum content – on issues such as school values, pastoral care, the responsibilities pupils can acquire and the extra-curricular opportunities they provide. It is these 'extra' things that you might want to think about, with your child, when you are considering which school will best suit them. You can use the following checklist to help explore these 'extras':

For pupils

✓ **Extra-curricular opportunities** – what opportunities does the school offer outside of lessons?

✓ **Pupils' voice** – how much say do pupils have about decisions made in school that affect them? Can the school tell you about something that changed as a result of pupils' 'voice'?

✓ **Responsibilities** – what positions of responsibility are available for pupils in school?

✓ **Pastoral care** – what support is available to pupils if they have any worries or health concerns?

✓ **Anti-bullying** – how clear are the arrangements for preventing and dealing with bullying?

✓ **Transition from primary to secondary** – what efforts does the school make to help pupils settle in when they first arrive?

✓ **Special educational or learning needs** – how does the school accommodate these?

✓ **Punishments** – when a pupil misbehaves, what punishments does the school issue and what does it do to address underlying causes of difficult behaviours?

✓ **Creativity** – how does the school encourage creativity?

✓ **Aspirations** – how does the school encourage its pupil to develop aspirations for their futures?

✓ **Academic achievement** – how well does the school do in terms of exam results? Does it perform better in some subjects than others?

✓ **Subject areas** – are there any curriculum areas that get more focus than others, for example, music, physical activity, drama?

✓ **Different subjects** – what subjects are on offer that might not be found in every school, for example, certain languages, sports, social sciences or arts subjects such as pottery, drama, theatre skills, photography and so on.

✓ **The school environment** – what efforts have been made to make the school environment pleasant? Is the dining experience an enjoyable one for pupils?

Beyond school

✓ **Parents/carers involvement in school** – how are parents/carers kept informed about activities in school? Are parents encouraged to be part of their child's learning and experiences at school? If so, how? What are the key methods of communication between parents/carers and the school?

✓ **Community involvement** – what does the school do in partnership with the community, for example, fundraising, work experience, inviting visitors in, signposting pupils to support available outside school?

Making a decision and staying positive

The idea of 'maximisers' and 'sufficers' is a concept stolen from marketing and it explains two different approaches to making decisions (or purchases in the case of marketing). In choosing a child's school some of us will research every last detail and find out as much as possible about the schools available before we feel we can make a decision (maximisers). Some of us will find out a little and make our decision based on the idea that the school is 'good enough' (sufficers).

Whichever decision-making style you naturally adopt there will always be an element of your child's experience of secondary school being influenced by their attitude towards the school. Be careful not to give your child pre-conceived ideas about any of the schools you are considering as failing to get into their 'first choice' of school might result in them attending a school they have heard a lot of bad things about.

If your child does not get into your first choice school, focus on the positive aspects of the place they will be going to. All schools have strong points!

13

Preparing for the move

The first thing to do is put any anxieties you have into perspective. Worrying about your child seems to be well and truly part of being a parent. Even those of us who are pretty laid back can still muster up anxiety for lots of things when it comes to our children. However, a lot of the worrying is almost definitely unfounded. Most people can remember things they did as a child or teenager that they would shudder to imagine their children doing now. But we survived didn't we?

Before you start

Moving to secondary school might well be a testing time for your child but statistically the most likely long-term outcome is that they will be perfectly fine. This is not to say you shouldn't support your child, but ultimately it will be your child who experiences the move and no amount of worrying on your part will help. Your child might well be anxious, but they do not want to be dealing with your worry as well!

Try to separate your own anxieties from those of your child. There's a danger that you might project your own worries on to your child over issues that they are perfectly fine with. Try not to jump to conclusions about what your child is thinking or worrying about.

What you might be thinking

What your child is thinking!

Schools have changed

Unless you have a job in education, you might assume that schools are the same as when you went to one. The good news is, they've changed! And in terms of looking after pupils' wellbeing, certainly changed for the better. This is as a result of legislation and an increasing awareness and understanding about promoting emotional health and well-being. Schools do differ of course, but you don't usually have to look far to see that progress has been made.

Anxieties you might have about secondary schools might now be irrelevant as schools may well have addressed them.

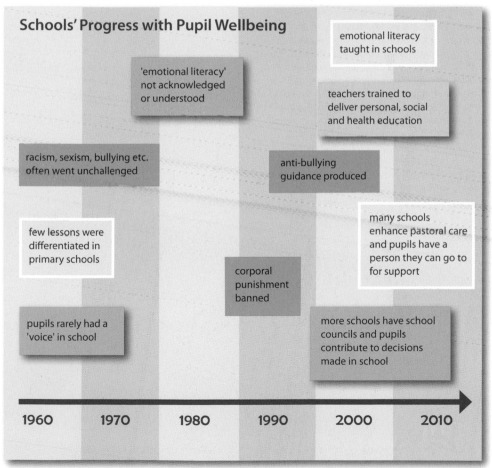

Schools' Progress with Pupil Wellbeing

emotional literacy taught in schools

'emotional literacy' not acknowledged or understood

teachers trained to deliver personal, social and health education

racism, sexism, bullying etc. often went unchallenged

anti-bullying guidance produced

many schools enhance pastoral care and pupils have a person they can go to for support

few lessons were differentiated in primary schools

corporal punishment banned

pupils rarely had a 'voice' in school

more schools have school councils and pupils contribute to decisions made in school

| 1960 | 1970 | 1980 | 1990 | 2000 | 2010 |

What support will your child need?

Everyone is different and because of this, each child will experience transition to secondary school in a completely different way. Some might breeze through the whole process without a care in the world while others really struggle. Some might find it difficult to keep on top of homework, others might find making new friends difficult and others might simply find getting up earlier to travel a greater distance really testing. Some might settle in extremely quickly, others might take a bit longer.

Here are some ways in which children can be different and how these differences can affect how a child copes with transition. The relevant pages for finding advice for each issue are also given:

Some children worry more than others

Some people are wired up to worry more than others with higher levels of neuroticism. This is why some children will simply feel more anxious than others during the transition process.

• If your child is a worrier, your support will be crucial. If your child worries to the point of not sleeping well, help them by talking things through, putting things into perspective and teach them some relaxation techniques.

 (See 'How is secondary school different from primary school?' on page 22, and 'Dealing with change' on page 26.)

• If your child rarely worries about anything, they might not be concerned about taking unnecessary risks. You could explore the idea of peer pressure and safety with them.

 (See 'Peer pressure and influence' on page 31 and 'Risk-taking behaviours – how to approach them' on page 86.)

Some children like to make and stick to plans and be organised, others are more adaptable, flexible and spontaneous

Organisation is not a trait commonly associated with the teenage years and this is for good reason. The physiological changes teenagers experience in their brains as well as their bodies can mean that being systematic and organised does not come naturally – even to a child that seemed that way in their childhood.

• If your child is prone to being disorganised focus on tools to help them to plan and think ahead, avoid distraction and stay motivated. Think about safety when it comes to your child's new journey to school.

(See 'A new route to school' on page 36, 'Becoming more organised' on page 44, 'Motivation' on page 66 and 'Keeping safe out and about' on page 91.)

• If your child likes to make plans and stick to them, then it might help them to talk through what to expect at secondary school.

(See 'How is secondary school different from primary school?' on page 22.)

Some children are outgoing and highly sociable and others are quiet and reflective

If your child is very sociable, they will hopefully find it easy to make new friends at secondary school. Other children have fewer friendships but they can be equally important.

• If your child is highly sociable, you could talk about the influence of peers.

(See 'Peer pressure and influence' on page 31.)

• If your child is slow to make friends, try focusing on making friends.

(See ('Making new friends – handy tip' on page 28 and 'Showing an interest in their new friends' on page 46.)

However, some children need to be organised and are only comfortable when they feel in control while others are completely comfortable with chaos and spontaneity. It is a spectrum and those at the 'organised end' will struggle less with the increased need to plan ahead while those at the flexible end might adapt more quickly to all the changes a new school brings.

Some children are more assertive than others

Some children are very good at sticking up for themselves and others, other children are not.

• If your child is not overly assertive, try teaching them some assertiveness skills.

(See 'Being assertive' on page 32.)

Some children are more sensitive to people's comment than others

Some children are more prone to taking things personally and becoming upset than others.

- If your child is sensitive to other people's comments, it can really help to teach them how to re-frame other people's comments and the method of 'fogging'.

  (See 'Being assertive' on page 32 and 'Developing emotional literacy' on page 92.)

Most children are practical and 'down to earth' but some are more imaginative and 'away with the fairies'

Children who are imaginative and 'away with the fairies' are more likely to struggle with day to day practicalities and being observant than those that are more 'down to earth'.

- If your child is prone to having their 'head in the clouds' try discussing ideas which will help them become more organised and consider the new route your child will take to school.

  (See 'Becoming more organised' on page 44 and 'A new route to school' on page 36.)

Talk about your own experiences

One way to start conversations with your child is to talk about your own experiences of leaving primary school and going to secondary school. You can do this in the light of having understood that schools have changed for the better over the years. Children usually love to hear stories of their parents' younger days. The following questions might help prompt such a conversation:

- What subjects did you like and not like when you were at secondary school? Why?

- Were there any particular teachers you really liked or any you did not like? Why?

- What rumours did you hear about secondary school before you went there and did they turn out to be true?

- Can you remember how you felt about starting secondary school when you were at primary school?

- How long did it take before you felt like you had settled in?

- How did you cope with having more homework?

- Did you make lots of new friends at secondary school or did you tend to stick with those that came with you from primary school?

- Do you have any funny stories from your time at secondary school?

- What did you like and dislike most about secondary school?

Finding out about the new school

The vast majority of schools make a fair amount of contact with the parents and carers of their future pupil intake before they start school. This is done through written communications (letters and school prospectuses) and sessions run in school that give information and an opportunity to answer parents' questions. This communication can be an opportunity for you to find out about the secondary school and its procedures that your child should know before they start – as some of their worries will be about not knowing what to do or how things are done.

The following checklist includes questions you could ask about your child's secondary school before they start. Most primary schools will gather much of this information for you and your child will be told some of it during visits. The secondary school will also provide you with a prospectus/information pack that will answer several of these questions. You might still like to go through this information with your child if you feel they would appreciate it.

Questions you might ask...

Keeping parents/carers informed

- How are parents kept informed about what is happening in school and if there are any concerns about their child?
- What procedures are in place for parents to communicate with the school?

Non-academic support for pupils

- If a child is worried, upset, being bullied or struggling with school in any way, what provision is made to support the child?

Support with school work

- If a child is finding their school work difficult, is any support provided?

Settling in

- What does the school do to help the new pupils settle in?

Anti-bullying

- What is the school's anti-bullying policy?
- How does a pupil report bullying and what happens if bullying is reported?

Special or medical needs

- If a child has any special or medical needs, who in school is informed of this and how are the child's needs accommodated?

School clubs

- What extra-curricular activities will be on offer for new pupils?

School rules

- What school rules and punishments will pupils need to be aware of?

Details about the school day

The first day

◆ Where will new pupils enter the school and go to when they arrive on their first day and what should they expect?

◆ How does the school help pupils to find their way around when they first arrive at the school?

Journey to and from school

◆ If a pupil travels to and from school by foot, bicycle, bus or is dropped off by car is there any information that child needs to know about how they enter the school – where they park their bike and so on.

Registration

◆ Where are pupils registered and what is the role of the person that registers them? For example, form tutor, pastoral support, stays with them throughout their time at the school and so on.

Timetable

◆ When does the school day start and finish?

◆ What will their timetable look like?

◆ How long are their lessons?

◆ When and how long are their breaks and lunch times?

Storage of personal items

◆ Are pupils provided with a place to keep their personal possessions, such as a locker?

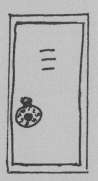

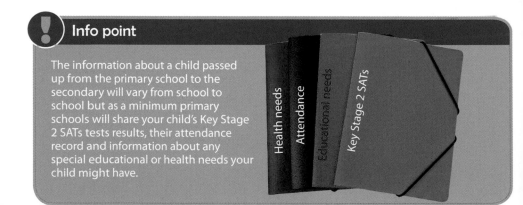

Info point

The information about a child passed up from the primary school to the secondary will vary from school to school but as a minimum primary schools will share your child's Key Stage 2 SATs tests results, their attendance record and information about any special educational or health needs your child might have.

Health needs

Attendance

Educational needs

Key Stage 2 SATs

Details about lessons

Curriculum

★ Are there any new subjects that pupils will have that they did not come across at primary school? For example – a new language, metalwork, woodwork, philosophy, new sports, science split into biology, chemistry and physics?

★ How has the school ensured that the curriculum carries on suitably from what the pupils learnt at primary school?

★ In what ways is the teaching at secondary school different from primary school – if it IS?

Homework

★ Approximately how much homework can each pupil expect to receive in each subject each week?

★ What happens If a pupil fails to complete a homework task?

★ Is there support available for pupils who are struggling with a particular piece of homework?

Grouping

★ How will pupils be grouped for different subjects?

★ Will pupils spend the majority of time with the same group of pupils or be jumbled up in every lesson?

★ Will pupils be grouped with some of their friends from primary school?

Specific equipment needed

★ What is the acceptable school uniform?

★ What jewellery, footwear and so on does the school allow?

★ What are the PE kit requirements?

★ What will pupils be expected to bring to school each day (e.g. writing materials)?

★ Are there any other extra bits of equipment needed and does the school provide them at a low cost? For example, scientific calculators, sketch books and so on.

★ What lunch facilities does the school offer (e.g. is there a canteen? What are the prices? What is the method of payment?)

★ What provision is made for those that have packed lunches?

You can use this checklist to explore what your child knows after they have attended an induction day. Note down any information that you feel your child still needs to know and request this from their primary or the secondary school. It is also a useful prompt to explore:

• what causes your child concern

• what things your child is looking forward to

• anything that surprised them.

How is secondary school different from primary school?

Every school is unique and therefore so are the exact changes a child will experience when they transfer. However, the following is an explanation of changes that most children will experience at this time of transition.

Teachers and lesson styles

In a typical primary school, your child will have spent most of the school week with one, two or possibly three different teachers. The relationship children have with their primary school teacher is usually one of significant familiarity. At secondary school, however, they will spend considerably less time with each of their different subject teachers. They might have some teachers for only an hour or two a week. These teachers will also teach a far larger number of pupils than their primary school colleagues and for that reason are likely to know the children they teach less well.

Experiencing a greater number of different teachers will mean children have to get used to a variety of teaching styles – some of which might be quite different from those they experienced at primary school. Again, this will depend on the philosophies of both the primary and secondary schools your child attends but approaches can be different in terms of:

- how much your child is expected to take responsibility for their own learning

- how often your child will be expected to work independently

- the balance between what is done in school and what is expected to be completed at home

- how many different teaching and learning approaches are adopted in any subject by the teachers, for example:

  - problem solving
  - drama
  - poster making
  - discussion
  - paired work
  - answering given written questions
  - filling in missing words on a worksheet
  - note taking
  - use of visual prompts
  - listening to teacher input or watching demonstrations
  - cross-curricular opportunities (topic work that covers more than one subject area)
  - using a text book
  - independent research opportunities
  - writing essays
  - self assessment
  - rote learning
  - how information technology is used in lessons.

The subjects

This does vary from school to school but the chances are your child will encounter a new subject or two. These might include:

- new sports
- a new modern foreign language
- design and technology split into further subjects, such as woodwork, metalwork, pottery, textiles, food design and technology
- science split into physics, biology and chemistry (although some schools do leave this until pupils are in their third or fourth year)
- citizenship
- philosophy/life skills/learning skills
- humanities spilt into geography, history, sociology and so on.

If your child's primary school taught lessons in a very cross-curricular way (i.e. taught a topic in which maths, literacy, geography, history and other subjects were covered), you child will experience a significant change as each subject at secondary school is usually taught separately.

More challenging work

Because of the greater variation in subjects, teaching styles and increased expectations due to learning progression, your child might discover that some subjects are more challenging than others.

Grouping

This varies from school to school but pupils are likely to be grouped according to ability – more than they were at primary school. This can, in some schools, mean that pupils spend different lessons with different pupils although most schools tend to keep this to a minimum in the first years of secondary school.

Compared to primary school where your child will have mostly been in the same class with the same children, your child will come across a greater number of fellow pupils.

More homework

There will be an increase in the volume of homework probably from a wider range of subjects once your child gets to secondary school.

Having a form tutor

Before arriving at secondary school, children will have been allocated a form and form tutor. This is the teacher that usually registers

them every morning but is also likely to have a more general responsibility for looking after their progress and well-being. Form tutors' responsibilities do vary from school to school (and will be affected by each tutor's individuality) but typically he/she:

✓ is responsible for issuing daily information and notices to their tutor group/form

✓ answers any queries pupils might have about school events, procedures, policy and so on

✓ is the first person a pupil should turn to for help, support and advice

✓ is responsible for encouraging punctuality and attendance

✓ is a point of contact for parents/carers should they need to discuss an issue about their child

✓ liaises with the head of the year group about their tutor group – especially if there are any concerns about a pupil

✓ accompanies their tutor group to assemblies.

He/she might also:

✓ deliver some personal, social and health education (PSHE) lessons

✓ be aware of and perhaps monitor their tutor group's progress across the curriculum

✓ take responsibility for motivating the tutor group at the start of each day!

✓ discuss a thought for the day, set a puzzle or facilitate a discussion about an event in the media and so on.

At most primary schools your child's class teacher would have been responsible for all of the above and your child would have had access to their teacher throughout the school day. At secondary school your child will have less opportunity to access help and support from their form tutor. However, an increasing number of secondary schools now allocate at least one member of staff that pupils can access at any time for non-academic help and support.

New and bigger building

Most pupils move from a smaller primary to a much larger secondary school. This means there is much more space to familiarise themselves with. There is also a greater expectation at secondary school for pupils to find their own way to where they need to be.

In primary school your child will have spent the vast majority of the lesson time in the same classroom. At secondary school, your child is likely to travel to different classrooms for different subjects.

More equipment

Secondary schools tend to have more equipment than primary schools. This is certainly true in areas of the curriculum such as science, design and technology and physical activity.

Pupils might also be expected to provide more equipment to participate in lessons such as a scientific calculator, protractor and so on.

Storage of personal possessions

Storage of possessions is straightforward in primary school. Because pupils move around secondary schools to different classes, they can no longer keep their possessions in one classroom. Many pupils carry their property with them in their school bag but schools usually provide some kind of lockable storage space for each pupil.

New procedures

Your child will have several new systems, routines and procedures to become familiar with. For example, systems for handing in homework, payment for lunches, routines for coming into school, new school rules, new punishments and so on. There is likely to be quite a bit of new information for your child to take in.

Lunch times

The procedure for payment, choosing meals and places to dine will be different from primary school. Many children express concern about familiarising themselves with this new procedure in particular.

Dealing with change

Life is never free from change. We feel secure with sameness and routine so change – whether it is through our own choosing or imposed upon us – can be unsettling. In experiencing change we can be fearful of the 'unknown' that is replacing our 'known'.

It is important to remember that change can also be very welcome as it can bring new and exciting opportunities.

Going to secondary school is a change imposed on our children. In some ways this makes it quite straightforward to deal with as it does not involve making a decision to do or not to do something. Coping with this big

change is therefore more about mindset than actions. If you can help your child to replace feelings of resistance and upset about change with acceptance and a commitment to it, they are likely to feel a lot less stressed about the whole thing.

Having said that, it is important to acknowledge that change can cause a range of powerful and conflicting emotions. The following 'graph' shows a typical emotional response to a change that is not a trauma or loss.

So in discussing the move to secondary with your child try to:

1 Stay positive and enthusiastic.

2 Present the move not as a problem but as an opportunity.

3 Give your child as much information about the new school as they need to reduce the amount of uncertainty and decrease the 'unknown' which can cause worry.

4 Be realistic about how unsettling change can be but also make it clear that there will be a time when the new will be familiar.

5 Discuss the idea that some of the worry about moving to secondary school is because it threatens our very basic need to belong and to feel safe and secure. Explain to your child that they will soon feel they belong and are safe in their new school, in just the same way as they did at primary school.

6 Remind your child of all the things that won't change during this time, for example, home life, family support, activities your child does out of school.

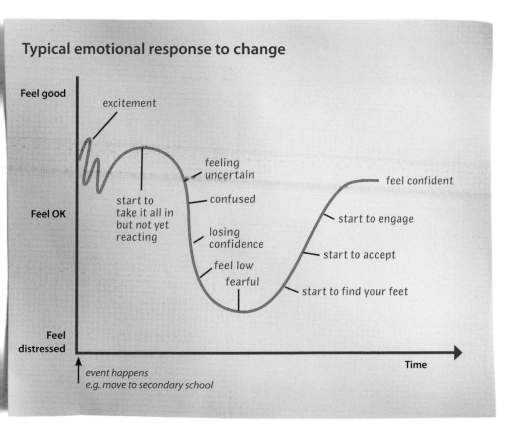

Typical emotional response to change

Feel good

excitement

Feel OK

start to take it all in but not yet reacting

feeling uncertain

confused

feel confident

losing confidence

start to engage

feel low

fearful

start to accept

start to find your feet

Feel distressed

Time

event happens
e.g. move to secondary school

A fresh start

A new school can create the opportunity for a fresh start. Part of this could be your child choosing to try that bit harder to either overcome things they found difficult at primary school or to change their attitude towards school. Even if your child breezed through primary school, transition can still provide a chance to take stock and work out what they hope to achieve at secondary school.

To consider the chance for a fresh start ask your child to reflect upon the issues in the table opposite.

Making new friends

Secondary school presents a great opportunity to make new friends. But, much like walking into a room full of strangers for some adults, this can prove to be daunting for some children. The following advice could help your child feel more at ease:

1 Remember everyone is in the same boat and probably feeling equally nervous. If one person seems very confident on the surface, it doesn't necessarily mean that's what they are feeling like inside!

2 Don't wait for others to talk to you. Make the effort to start up conversations. Everyone appreciates a bit of friendliness – however 'cool' they might appear. You could begin by asking straightforward questions such as:

> • Which primary school did you go to?
>
> • Do you live near to this school?
>
> • Have you got an older brother or sister at this school?
>
> • Did you have a nice summer holiday?
>
> • Were you looking forward to coming here?

3 If you are in a class with some children from your primary school, don't just talk to them. Make the effort to include children who came from other schools.

4 Give everyone a chance. Don't make assumptions about someone based on what they look like or how they seem at first.

5 Nobody gets on with absolutely everyone. It will take a little time to find the people who will become really good friends.

6 Remember to treat others how you would like to be treated. Friendly behaviour includes:

✓ making eye contact and smiling

✓ being chatty and asking other people about themselves

✓ listening carefully to what others say

✓ giving compliments

✓ offering to help others, for example, holding a door open for someone

✓ asking people if they would like to join in with something and make sure everyone feels included

✓ not being bossy – asking rather than demanding

✓ laughing at people's jokes

✓ joining in and making sure you are part of whatever is happening and not deliberately sitting on your own.

Issue	Is this something you could consider improving? (tick)	What I think I could do to improve.
Getting to school on time		
Remembering to take the things I need to school		
Handing homework in on time		
Listening well in lessons		
Trying to complete more work in lessons		
Asking for help if I need it		
Worrying less about what other people think about me		
Supporting my friends		
Keeping a positive attitude towards school		
Being friendly and kind towards others		
Getting really fit		
Taking part in more extra-curricular activities		
Being determined to try harder in lessons I least like: (list these lessons here) • • •		
Tackle the things I often get told off for – so that they're no longer a problem. (list these things here) • • •		

Changing relationships

In moving to secondary school many children start to place a greater importance upon their relationships with friends. This is partly because they are moving from a school where one adult played a very key role in their day-to-day existence to a school where they see many more adults for a shorter time and so know them less well. (It's no surprise, therefore, that their friends and peers step up to become more significant in their lives.) But this shift in focus is also just part of growing up and a natural progression to increasingly looking away from family life towards new opportunities, experiences and relationships. It is a healthy development that will ultimately help your child become more independent.

This progression can, however, leave some parents and carers feeling a little out of control and out of touch with their child's life. Now is the time to remember the solid foundations you laid in your child's early life and to start trusting your child with slowly increasing degrees of freedom and independence – within safe and clearly spelt out limits!

As friends start to have a bigger impact on your child's life they will become more vulnerable to peer influence and pressure. This can have both good and bad outcomes! It is a good idea to discuss both peer influence and pressure with your child before they attend secondary school so that they are aware of it and can spot the dangers. Teaching your child to be assertive can also help (see page 32).

Peer pressure and influence

Your child is far more likely to do something as a result of peer influence than peer pressure. The image of one child pressurising another into trying a cigarette is often used as an example of peer pressure but in reality, very few children will experience this situation. Your child would be far more likely to start smoking, for example, just because they believe it is what everyone else is doing and/or what everyone thinks is 'cool' or rebellious.

If you help your child understand that our peers can affect our behaviour, you can help them resist this influence if they need to. You could explain that:

- Doing something just because you think everyone else is doing it is not a good reason.

- Everyone admires a person who sticks up for themselves and only does things because they really want to. It is admirable to always be true to yourself.

- It can sometimes take confidence to be different (or think you are being different).

- Teasing someone for being different is nasty and can be seen as bullying.

- We all like to feel we belong and fit in with our peers. We can believe in and enjoy different things but still have great friendships with them. While it can be great to have things in common with friends, it would be a very boring world if all our friends were exactly the same as us. True friends respect or even admire differences.

handy tip Peer influence and pressure doesn't make people just do bad things and does'nt just affect children and teenagers. Consider what happens if someone who has been drinking a considerable amount of alcohol declares in front of a room of adults that they are going to drive home.

Info point

Peer – a person of equal standing as you. In other words, for your child, a friend, an acquaintance or any other school-aged child.

Peer pressure – when someone is pressurised into doing something by a peer!

The result of **peer influence** is that someone does something just because everyone else is doing it or they think everyone else is doing it.

- If you ever find yourself in a situation where someone is trying to persuade you to do something dangerous or simply something you don't want to do – you will probably be admired if you don't give in to their pressure. Sometimes assertively stating that you do not want to do something can be enough to stop someone from pressurising you.

- Ask yourself why you are doing something and if you really want to do it. If your answer is that you're doing it just because you're scared of what others might think then chances are, you don't really want to do it.

Being assertive

Being assertive doesn't always work but it has more chance of getting you out of an unwanted situation than any other approach. Teaching your child how to be assertive can be a life-lesson well learned and will equip them to handle tricky situations better. If you already model assertiveness, the chances are they will already understand it!

The table below, however, can be used to help explain assertiveness to your child and its advantages over other approaches.

PASSIVE	ASSERTIVE	AGGRESSIVE
O.K. then whatever you say I will	I don't want to do that thank you No I won't do that but I can help you out with something else if you want	Grrrrrr Go away - you're horrible I hate you

PASSIVE	**ASSERTIVE**	**AGGRESSIVE**
Gives in and ends up doing something they don't want to	**States what they want to happen while still showing respect for the other person**	**'Attacks' and makes the other person feel bad or angry**

Suppose another person was trying to persuade you to do something you didn't want to do, such as climb on a roof. Here are three possible ways of responding:

The passive way

'Ok' and then you climb on the roof.
Not good because:

→ You end up doing what you didn't want to do.

→ You look like you could be persuaded to do anything and other people might decide they can boss you around too.

→ Climbing on a roof is dangerous and you could get hurt.

The aggressive way

In an angry voice: 'You're really stupid and bossy'.
Not good because:

→ It might make the other person angry and therefore escalate the situation and possibly end up in a fight.

→ You might make yourself open to being teased because you have lost your temper or become upset.

→ If someone is a bit of a bully, they are more likely to get pleased about getting an emotional response from you than if they don't and this can make them carry on.

The assertive way

In a calm voice: and good eye contact with the person you are speaking to: 'I don't want to climb on the roof thank you'.
Good because:

→ You haven't shown an emotional response and therefore have not opened yourself up to further teasing.

→ You have shown respect towards the other person and therefore given them no real reason to become angry so things do not become emotionally charged and escalate.

→ You state clearly what you want to happen and you don't climb on the roof and therefore remain safe.

Fogging is a useful approach to adopt if you are being teased as it is about giving a very unexpected response. This usually catches out the person who is teasing and they therefore become lost for words! It is best illustrated by example:

You're useless at that.

(Casually) Yes I know, let's hope I get better hey!

The teaser did not get the emotional or irritated response they were expecting and the teasing is likely to stop.

Support networks

At a time of change such as moving to secondary school it is especially important that your child knows exactly where to go for help – while at school and at home.

In many cases it might be you that offers this support but as your child grows up and becomes more independent, they are increasingly likely to turn to other people. You may feel uncomfortable about this but the important thing is that your child receives support rather than who they get it from.

To help your child become more aware of their support network, compose a list of responsible adults (other than yourself) who your child feels they could go to for help, support or advice. To prompt such a list you could ask:

Who would you turn to if...

? you had fallen out badly with a friend?

? you were struggling with school work?

? you had an argument with your parent/carer?

? you had a crush on someone and needed to talk about it?

? you felt you weren't fitting in or you felt lonely?

handy tip

Feeling up and feeling down. It is quite normal for anyone to feel happy at times and down at others. That is normal life. However, if someone feels miserable for a long period of time, the chances are they need some help. A person might also need help if they:

☹ think the same thought over and over

☹ cry a lot

☹ can't sleep well

☹ have feelings of dread or nervousness

☹ don't feel like doing something they usually love doing

☹ don't feel safe.

? you were worried about something to do with your body and/or your health?

? you were being bullied?

Often it will be friends who provide support but make it clear that sometimes, in more serious situations (such as being bullied) an adult will need to be told because it would be difficult for a friend alone to sort this out.

The kind of people your child might turn to are:

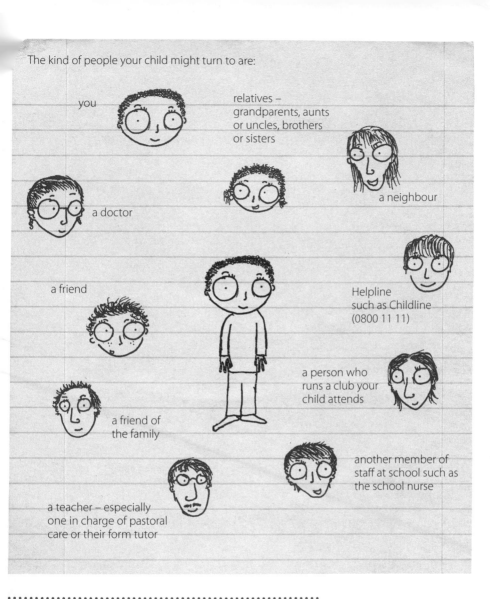

you

relatives –
grandparents, aunts
or uncles, brothers
or sisters

a neighbour

a doctor

a friend

Helpline
such as Childline
(0800 11 11)

a person who
runs a club your
child attends

a friend of
the family

another member of
staff at school such as
the school nurse

a teacher – especially
one in charge of pastoral
care or their form tutor

handy tip

Asking for help is sometimes perceived as
a weakness, especially for boys because
they are more likely to receive that
message from family, friends and society
generally. It is important to point out
that everyone needs help at different times in their
life and it's always much better to ask for help than
suffer in silence. Asking for help until you get it is
always the smart thing to do.

A new route to school

For most children, secondary school will mean a new route to school and often a slightly longer journey. It's very important to get your child familiar with their new route. Sadly, statistics show a rise in road traffic accidents around the time when children have just started at secondary school. This rise is probably due to several factors such as:

- unfamiliarity with the new route

- the journey is often longer

- children paying more attention to friends they travel with than to potential dangers

- travelling by a new means e.g. cycling, bus

- the clocks going back in October – so some pupils travel home in the dark if they have attended after-school clubs.

In preparing your child for their new journey, it can be hugely beneficial to take them on a 'dummy run'. On this run show them bus stops, point out the safest places to cross the roads and any other potential hazards, such as narrow paths, cycle paths or bad places to cross because of inability to see well. If the route is complicated or if there is a choice of routes, use a map to help your child become familiar with the roads between their home and school. If possible, arrange for your child to go to school with another child who lives close by.

handy tip

If your child is cycling to school ensure that they have passed their cycling proficiency as it provides them with sound safety awareness and rules of the road!

School uniform

Your child might be quite excited about getting a whole new school uniform (and PE kit) and might appreciate making a day of buying it. The following advice might seem obvious, but is still useful:

★ Even if your child can't wait to kit themselves out in their new uniform after leaving primary school, wait until late August/early September before buying. Your child is probably growing at a rate of knots and one month's growth can be significant!

★ Buy big! If your child is on the cusp of two sizes always go for the larger as they will grow into it in no time. A parent/carer never really needs to be told this!

★ If money is tight, look to friends to see if any hand-me-downs are available. Alternatively the secondary school might sell off second-hand uniforms cheaply or provide help with finances. You could start the first year of the new school with a brand new uniform but once the novelty has warn off be on the look-out for second-hand uniforms.

School bag

However much your child might ask for a fancy or stylish bag in the shop, they will probably be grateful if you insist that the school bag they get is practical. This will mean it needs to be waterproof, able to be zipped up, large enough for several books so they are not crumpled and possibly extra side pockets for money, notes and any other small things they need to find easily.

Extra pieces of equipment

The secondary school will inform you about any further equipment your child might need. There is usually an expectation that they will arrive with some basic stationery (in a pencil case) but they might also need a scientific calculator and other bits and pieces such as art sketchbooks. Some children can become anxious if they don't have everything they need so do a double check!

The school website

One really useful resource for preparing your child for secondary school is the school's website. Take time to explore this with your child. This will not only help you share information about the new school but it will also demonstrate your interest in their new venture.

School websites do vary but hopefully you will find some things of interest. Some schools' websites include a screen or two for new pupils which aim to help them feel positive about coming to the school.

Starting secondary school

The closer the first day looms and once the 'back to school' signs pop up everywhere thoughts of secondary school are likely to be rattling around in your child's head. They might appear completely unfazed but chances are they will be thinking something about it. They could be excited; sad the summer holiday is coming to an end; feeling uncertain about it all; worried generally; anxious about certain details or a combination of all of these.

Feelings are feelings!

Many people have experienced being told that they have no right to be angry or they have been teased for being too sensitive. This can sometimes result in people suppressing, ignoring or overly apologising for feeling the way they do – but the feeling is still real and is being experienced. It will still have an impact somewhere one way or another! Feelings are feelings and none of us have control over them so nobody can be told they have no right to feel what they feel. (However, people do have a choice about how they behave as a result of their feelings.)

Always take your child's feelings seriously and never mock them for feeling that way. What might seem like a trivial thing to you (with your lifetime's accumulation of wisdom and hindsight!) might feel all-consuming for your child. The best thing you can do is always lend a supportive and earnest ear! Think back to your teenage years. Most people would agree that they felt most things more intensively back then than they do now, not less.

A nice way of gently broaching the subject of starting at a new school is to review the whole of the summer holiday with your child as it comes close to finishing. One way of doing this is by using an emotion graph. Try reproducing a version of this graph on a large sheet of paper so you can lengthen it horizontally.

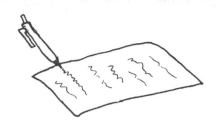

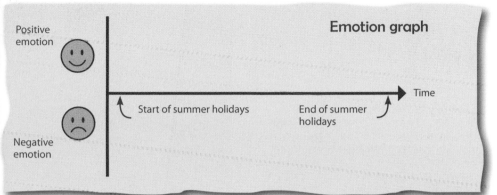

Start by asking your child to list the main events they can remember from just before, during and towards the end of the holidays. For example: day trips, having friends over, visiting family, swimming, events within a holiday away, parties and so on. Try to place them in the correct time order (don't worry if it's not exact).

Next take a pen and start the 'graph' just before term ended at primary school and ask your child to recall how they were feeling at that time. Ask them to draw a line to represent positive and negative emotions they experienced at the different times and label what caused them. See the example below:

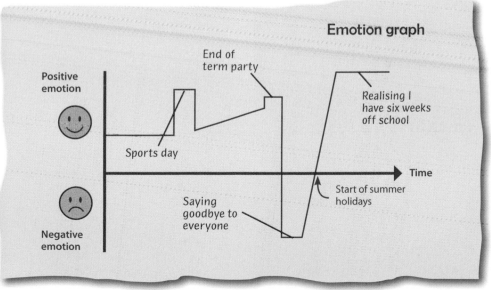

Continue the graph using the line to indicate whether their memory of each event in the holidays caused a positive or negative emotion. Take the graph right to the end of the holidays and then ask your child to anticipate how they think they will feel the night before they start back and the early days of secondary school.

handy tip

'Emotion graphs' are an effective way to explore (and prompt discussions about) your child's responses to recent events at any time. They can also be used to talk about the day they've just experienced.

Hopefully this activity will start conversations about how your child is feeling about going to a new school and you can address any specific worries (using the different sections in this book) or tackle the issue of feeling worried generally. The following notes can help with this.

A word about worrying

Worry can be defined as thinking a thought that is not at all useful over and over again. Worrying does not achieve anything except to make you feel bad. It is also true that some people are wired up to be bigger worriers than others.

People tend to worry about something that is going to happen in the future – which they are unsure of. Because they are worrying about the future, they have no way of knowing how things will actually turn out. This often means the worrying is about something that could well turn out to be fine. In fact, most changes that we worry about (such as changing schools) can be worse in anticipation than reality! Often when we get to the point in the future that caused us to worry earlier, we wonder what all the fuss was about!

When we are worried about something it is important to separate the things we can do something about from the things we cannot do anything about. As a lot of worrying is about things that have not yet happened – the chances are, a lot of our worries are about something we can do nothing about – not at this point in time anyway.

Use the checklist 'How is secondary school different from primary school?' on page 22 which outlines the changes you will experience to see if any are causing you more concern than others. The advice in this book can help you with specific worries – for the things that you can actually do something about!

...he night before

If your child does not sleep well when they are worried about something, take time during the evening before the first day to:

★ reassure them that even if they don't get a good night's sleep they will still be able to function the next day (and will get a better night's sleep the following night).

★ promise that this time tomorrow they will feel quite differently and realise the worrying was totally unnecessary.

★ discuss things they might like to think about to help them get to sleep, for example, recall a nice memory from the holiday or something dull – like picturing the layout and position of everything in your house on a visual tour or counting sheep of course!

★ Discuss a few simple relaxation techniques (see below).

Relaxation techniques for going to sleep

Tensing and relaxing

This is good if your body is full of tension. Really tense every muscle in your body and hold it for as long as is reasonably comfortable. On an 'out' breath relax every muscle into the bed. Repeat until you feel the tension has gone. If you hold stress in your neck – as many people do – try lifting you head up off the pillow on an 'in' breath, hold for several seconds and then sink back into the pillow on an 'out' breath.

Deep breathing

Breathing more deeply slows the heart rate and relaxes you. Take slower and deeper breaths as you lie on your back.

Simple visualisation linked to breathing

Visualise a circle with a small dot on it near the circumference that spins around from the centre. As you breathe in, visualise the dot smoothly moving up to the top and as you breathe out, visualise it moving round and down to the bottom. Try to spin the circle as smoothly as you can. This will hopefully empty your head of the worries as you focus on the dot.

Bit by bit

As you lie there, start with the feet and for each breath out imagine your foot relaxing and sinking further into the bed. Then move onto the ankles, then the knees and so on…

Of course getting lots of exercise in the day nearly always helps you to sleep well.

Make sure their bag is packed

On a practical level it's a good idea for your child to pack their school bag and make any arrangements about getting to school with friends the night before term starts at the latest. The content of their bag will probably need to include:

- ✓ a break time snack and drink
- ✓ packed lunch or lunch money
- ✓ pencil case
- ✓ any homework tasks they were set on the induction day
- ✓ mobile phone – if the school allows them.

Your child is unlikely to need their PE kit on the first day and before they have been issued with a locker they might not appreciate carrying it around all day.

The early days

When you wake up on the morning of the start of term, hopefully there will be very little to have to think about. If your child is travelling with friends, make sure they leave in plenty of time to meet them as nobody wants to be late on the first day. If your child is going alone or if you are dropping them off, suggest they stand outside the school gate until someone they know comes along. They can then walk in with that person and won't be on their own. Also if your child is walking alone suggest that if they are unsure of which way to go, they could follow some of the many other pupils that are bound to be walking in the direction of the school.

Be sure your child knows where they are meant to go once they are in school on that first day.

Ups and downs

As the graph in 'Coping with change' on page 27 shows, your child is likely to experience ups and downs in those early days at secondary school as they:

1 learn secondary school is actually OK

2 find there are routines and lessons they love and those they are not so keen on

3 make new friends and decide others might not be such good friends

4 discover which teachers they like and which they don't

5 get used to a new routine of getting to school and coming home

6 forget a few things and then start to remember them!

Communication during the early days… and beyond

Some children tell all, some give away hardly anything and there's also everyone in-between. Showing an interest and being supportive might be seen as prying by some children but others will welcome it. You know your child and what they will tolerate!

For children who keep communication to a minimum you might like to:

- Tell your child that you will not ask lots of questions about school on the condition that if they become worried about anything – however small – they will come and tell you (or another adult) about it.

- Ask your child for a mark out of ten for the day they have just had – zero being awful, ten being great and then ask for reasons for their score.

- Have a notebook as a form of communication. Some children find it easier to communicate in writing. This notebook could be placed under their pillow once each of you has written in it. You can write questions about school or just generally about life, share information about your day and/or write silly questions that might make your child laugh, for example, which of the following 'skills' would you like your parents/carers to have: a) be a gourmet cook b) be able to fly a plane c) be unable to see mess or d) please specify.

- At some point in the evening – perhaps over an evening meal, ask everyone in the family to talk about the best and worst part of their day.

- On Sunday nights, check in with your child and ask them what they feel is going well and what is not. Explain that you will ask every Sunday for your own peace of mind!

- Talk to your child's friends. Quite often other people's children will communicate more readily with you than your own. They can often provide insight into what's going on at school and what is generally felt about it.

- If you have genuine concerns about anything to do with your child it is probably best to contact the school and make enquiries – preferably with your child's permission.

Getting lost in the new school

One of the most common things primary school children cite as a concern about secondary school is getting lost. Once there, however, pupils soon realise that this concern was exaggerated and unnecessary. The school will have made efforts to familiarise pupils with the new grounds and buildings so getting completely lost soon becomes extremely unlikely. This is not to say that children do not occasionally get confused but if they do someone is usually around to help and teachers are normally forgiving of lateness in the early days.

A couple of weeks into term and pupils can easily navigate themselves to all their lessons.

Becoming more organised

Settling in is likely to take less time than your child will have anticipated. You can guarantee with conviction that school will feel like 'just school' pretty quickly!

However, there will be a period of time when everything does feel new. Remind your child that there are a lot of new things to learn, remember and adjust to when you get to a new school and they can be forgiven for making a few mistakes and forgetting the odd thing in these early days. If they find they are persistently forgetting things, however they might need some help addressing this.

To help your child, sit with them one evening shortly after the start of secondary school, look at their timetable and construct a 'What you need to take' checklist for each day of the week. This will include anything that needs to be taken regularly on specific days of the week such as:

◆ homework

◆ particular text books

◆ PE kit.

Also construct a general checklist of things your child might like to check as they pack their school bag such as:

Checklist

- [ ] pencil case

- [ ] any homework due in that was not set on a regular day or that has been done prior to the deadline

- [ ] dinner money

- [ ] any letters or money due in

- [ ] wet weather clothing/sun cream

- [ ] anything needed for special events or activities (e.g. musical instrument)

- [ ] sports gear (e.g. swimming kit, particular footwear).

Rarely does anyone comment that a child heading for adolescence has suddenly become incredibly organised! There are so many physiological changes happening during puberty that they can feel like their body no longer fits and feel generally disorientated. It is therefore slightly unfortunate timing that moving to secondary school will require your child to take more initiative in organising themselves so they arrive with appropriate equipment, letters, books and homework on the right days. It is also rarely a rewarding role for any parent/carer to have to keep checking that their child has all the right 'stuff' each day. A balance between helping your child to organise themselves but also trusting them to do so is the best way forward.

Another thing that can help massively with organisation is to encourage your child to pack their bag the night before each school day. This avoids the mad panicked rush that many parents/carers are familiar with on school mornings and makes it much less likely that they will be late or forget things.

Showing an interest in their new friends

In the early days of secondary school your child will encounter and spend time with a lot of new people. (Advice about making friends can be found in 'helpful tips' on page 28.) In these early days, encourage your child to talk about the new people they meet and show enthusiasm for the whole idea that their circle of friends will become larger. Ask encouraging questions which show you are interested in the friends they have made, such as:

- ❓ How many lessons do you share with them?
- ❓ Do you sit next to them in any lessons?
- ❓ Where do they live?
- ❓ Which primary school did they come from?
- ❓ Have they got a good sense of humour?
- ❓ Do you feel comfortable with them?
- ❓ Have you contacted them on a social networking site?
- ❓ Can you see yourself socialising with them out of school?
- ❓ Could you start travelling to school with them?

It is also realistic, however, to acknowledge that your child will not necessarily like or get on with everyone (that's as true for children as it is for adults). We are all different and not likely to get on with everyone we meet.

Setting up homework routines

Homework is important, not only because it reinforces learning in class but mostly because it helps your child become good at independent working.

Hopefully, early on in the school term you will be made aware of how the school manages the setting and taking in of homework. Many schools use some kind of homework diary but if your child's school does not, ask them for a copy of their homework policy so you are sure about what happens.

Show an interest in your child's homework, offer some support and have high expectations of their achievement. If you do this they are more likely to become successful and independent learners and develop good working habits. Also try to do the following:

1 Provide a quiet space, free from distraction, where your child can complete their homework.

2 Provide a homework equipment box in this space. This should contain pencils, an eraser, a sharpener, ruler, calculator, scrap paper, scissors, a glue stick, protractor, compass, dictionary, thesaurus etc.

3 Discuss the idea of a good homework routine. Doing homework just before going to bed is far from ideal. If your child attends after-school clubs or activities there may need to be some flexibility with this routine. You might suggest that they have a brief rest when they first get home from their school day – just time for a drink and a snack – and then do their homework.

4 Show an interest in your child's work (even if you don't find it particularly interesting) as this will help with motivation.

5 Reward your child (e.g. with a choice of TV programme, a choice of dinner, a small treat) if they manage their homework independently and well. It is easy to overlook things when they run smoothly but it is also motivating if you acknowledge that you are impressed with their management of homework.

6 Explain that you will trust your child to work independently. Try not to hover over them as this will be distracting and give the message that you don't trust them to get on with it. They are used to working on their own at school so shouldn't struggle too much to do so at home.

For advice on tackling homework problems see 'Dealing with homework' on page 64.

Sleep

There is plenty of research that proves that a sleep-deprived child will struggle to learn – as even a little bit less sleep than is needed can affect your ability to think properly and respond quickly. Make sure you child is getting enough sleep – especially during this time of adjustment to their new school. At the age of 12 this needs to be somewhere between nine and eleven hours per night.

A new routine

Getting up at a different time; getting to school a different way; having more homework; taking part in new after-school activities; remembering what to take to school each day; getting used to new teachers/lessons and needing to be more organised will soon settle into a routine that your child can hopefully manage independently. After a few weeks, you can check how well they have adjusted using the following true/false quiz.

Hopefully your child's responses will indicate that they have started to settle in and feel part of their new school. If there are any particular issues they are struggling with, their responses to these statements will highlight these.

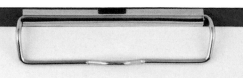

How's it all going quiz

Do you think each statement is true or false?.................................. **TRUE** **FALSE**

- The school still feels really new.. ☐ ☐
- I often get lost in school.. ☐ ☐
- I am scared of the older children in school............................... ☐ ☐
- I am finding the work too difficult... ☐ ☐
- Going to secondary school is very different from going to primary school. .... ☐ ☐
- I have made some new friends... ☐ ☐
- I like break times.. ☐ ☐
- I like lunch times. .... ☐ ☐
- I like my form tutor .... ☐ ☐
- I still get confused about what to do at lunch times. .... ☐ ☐
- I have got used to my new journey to school each morning. .... ☐ ☐
- I usually turn up to school with the right books and equipment needed for each day.. ☐ ☐
- I am worried about the amount of homework I am getting.. ☐ ☐
- I have got used to my new teachers and what they expect.. ☐ ☐
- I nearly always hand my homework in on time. .... ☐ ☐
- I always get to my lessons on time... ☐ ☐

Settling in

Once your child has well and truly settled into secondary school, got past those initial weeks and appears to be problem free, it's easy to forget to check that they are not struggling with anything. During the spring term many secondary schools do something to investigate what their pupils are thinking and feeling about their not-so-new school. Sometimes this involves parents/carers.

Spring term check up

Many of us are not very good at asking for help and it can often take a direct question from someone before we acknowledge that we might be finding something a bit difficult. You can use the 'check-up' prompts on the page opposite in the spring term to check that your child has settled in without any major problems and to get you talking about their general wellbeing.

If the results of the table indicate that your child is struggling with something at their new school, there is advice in this book giving advice about most potential problems. A quick chat with your child might be enough to make them feel better about a particular difficulty. Remember your child is often best placed to work out their own solution as they know all the details of the situation and will quickly be able to assess whether a particular solution 'suits' them and is likely to work.

Some problems however – such as bullying – will definitely need adult intervention. If a problem is serious, do not hesitate to contact the school and speak to a member of staff who is responsible for your child's welfare.

	☺	☺	☹	Strongly agree	Agree	Not sure	Disagree	Strongly disagree
I look forward to going to school most days.								
I can think of several friends that I like spending time with at secondary school.								
I understand most of the work I am set and I am able to do it.								
I do not get told off by the teachers at school.								
Homework is generally not a problem.								
If I was worried about something, I would know who to talk to for help and support.								
I get enough sleep in term time and do not feel tired.								
Nobody in the school has been really nasty to me.								
There are some lessons I really don't like.								
There are things we do at school that I really enjoy.								

The curriculum – some background knowledge

Year 7 is the start of Key Stage 3. The 'Key Stages' are a system schools use to organise and implement the curriculum. Key Stage 3 is Year 7, Year 8 and Year 9. At the end of Year 9 (usually) your child will make some choices about which non-compulsory subjects they want to keep and which they want to drop and other new subjects they might want to take up. The subjects they keep will be the ones they can take GCSE exams in.

Key Stage 3 therefore has a greater number of compulsory subjects than Key Stage 4 – including some which your child might not go on to study for exams.

Info point

Compulsory National Curriculum subjects in Key Stage 3 are:

★ **English***
(this can include drama)

★ **maths***

★ **science***
(some schools split this into biology, physics and chemistry)

★ **history**

★ **geography**

★ **design and technology**
(this can include food technology, metalwork, woodwork, etc)

★ **information and communication technology (ICT)***
(mostly computing)

★ **art and design**

★ **modern foreign languages**
(the languages on offer vary from school to school)

★ **music**

★ **citizenship***
(explores topics such as criminal justice, conflict, community, diversity, democracy, politics, economy, human rights, the media etc)

★ **physical education***

* These subjects remain compulsory at Key Stage 4.

Schools also have to provide:

- **Careers education and guidance** (in Year 9)

- **Religious education (RE)** – you have the right to withdraw your child from RE lessons.

- **Sex and relationship education (SRE).** The quality and quantity of SRE varies from school to school. As a parent/carer, you have the right to withdraw your child from SRE lessons (that are not part of the science statutory curriculum). Your child's school should let you know about its SRE programme (what will be covered and when) before it starts.

Many schools also provide:

- **Personal, social and health education (PSHE)** which covers topics such as healthy lifestyles, managing difficult feelings, developing self-esteem, safety, drug education and so on.

- Other lessons such as philosophy or learning skills.

Some schools might split compulsory subjects up and give them slightly different names. The school prospectus is likely to contain information about different subjects.

Your child will appreciate you showing an interest in their timetable and asking them questions about each teacher and how much they like each subject. You could start to ask about the subjects they might want to continue with in the future.

How do children learn best?

You can learn a lot from exploring your child's interests, strengths and passions and your child is likely to appreciate the interest you shown in them. A little self-awareness can be extremely helpful!

Use the following tools with your child to explore their preferences, strengths and interests and how they relate to their learning as well as choices available to them in the future.

VAK

Most people have a style of learning that suits them best. Many schools are very aware of the following model (VAK) for exploring ways in which children learn best:

- **Visual**

  We can learn most effectively through diagrams and having interesting visual prompts to look at or read.

- **Auditory**

  We can learn effectively by just listening and talking.

- **Kinaesthetic**

  We learn best by actually doing (or sometimes imagining doing) something and touching things and taking action.

Your child might already be able to tell you their VAK preference. Some school lessons are planned with these three learning preferences in mind.

There are free online tests that can be used to explore these preferences (put VAK into a search engine) but you can consider the following to work out what your preference might be.

1 If you were trying to find somewhere would you be more likely to prefer:

a being told the directions verbally? (**A**)

b looking at a map? (**V**)

c having a vague idea of where you are going and where the place is in relation to other places you know and following your instincts? (**K**)

2 If you were trying to assemble a tricky piece of equipment, would you rather:

a just have a go? (**K**)

b listen to clear instructions? (**A**)

c look at a diagram that shows you how to make it? (**V**)

3 If you were considering whether or not to go to a particular café to eat, would you rather:

a read online reviews about the cafe and look at photos of it (**V**)

b imagine the experience and decide whether it will be good (**K**)

c listen to what others have to say about the café (**A**)

4 If someone gives you directions to somewhere do you:

a remember the words that were said? (**A**)

b imagine a map being drawn of the route in your head? (**V**)

c actually imagine turning left and right and straight ahead and produce a three-dimensional image of your journey in your head? (**K**)

handy tip

Being aware of your preference can help you with your learning. For example, if you are a visual learner and a teacher expects you to listen to instructions, doodling a picture of what they are saying or taking notes will help you take in the information.

Multiple Intelligences

Psychologist Howard Gardner has argued for
some time that there are several different types
of intelligence and that many schools focus
on (and exams test) just two or three of these.
Quite often, after leaving school, people find
they use different intelligences in their jobs —
those that the curriculum mostly focused on.

Look at the chart on the opposite page and
consider which of the following intelligences
you think you have most of.

Type of intelligence	Are likely to be good at...	At school you are likely to be good at...
Linguistic	using words and language, writing, explaining things, understanding what words and phrases mean, languages	English, drama, discussing things, expressing yourself, explaining things to others, possibly modern foreign languages
Logical-mathematical	doing calculations, working out what causes things to happen, working out patterns, problem solving, mental arithmetic, logic puzzles	maths, science, design technology when it requires problem solving
Spatial/visual	imagining what things look like (2D and 3D), understanding pictures, map reading, working out 3D puzzles	map reading, art, design technology when it requires planning models etc
Musical	playing music, appreciating music and sound, performing music, composing music, recognising patterns, rhythms, pitch, tone and instruments in music you listen to	music, playing an instrument, analysing tunes
Bodily Kinaesthetic	movement, body control, using hands to make things, hand-eye coordinating, sport	physical activity, drama, anything that requires you to do or make something with your hands e.g. pottery, woodwork etc
Naturalist	recognising and categorising different things from nature, identifying animals, plants, birds etc, noticing and seeing visual differences and details in things	identifying things in science/biology
Interpersonal	understanding other people, getting on with other people, understanding other people's points of view	making friends, being sensitive to others, helping others
Intrapersonal	understanding yourself, self-awareness, know what causes your emotions and how best to respond	understanding your friendships and why you get on with certain people, being motivated to do things

Looking at qualities

The tool opposite can be used not only to help your child become more self-aware but also gives you an opportunity to praise their strengths.

Either:

Take all or some of the following qualities one at a time. Make sure your child understands what the quality means and then both you and your child can give a mark out of ten for how much you think they have that particular quality (zero means not at all, ten means a quality they have a lot of). Once a mark has been given, compare answers and discuss! To make it a positive exercise select qualities you feel your child will only get a reasonably high score for.

Or

Ask your child to choose the five qualities out of those listed they think most describe them. You could do the same exercise for your child and see if you picked any of the same qualities.

Your child might like to repeat the exercise for you!

Be aware that most qualities have an opposite that could also be considered a quality. For example one person might make plans and stick to them – another might not and their strength would be that they are flexible!

Qualities to think about:

		marks out of 10
★	Good at listening	
★	Organised	
★	Willing to be helpful	
★	Remembers things	
★	Trustworthy	
★	Good at planning	
★	Polite	
★	Energetic	
★	Not lazy	
★	Enthusiastic	
★	Friendly	
★	Sensible	

		marks out of 10
☺	Determined to get things done	
☺	Generous	
☺	Optimist	
☺	Imaginative	
☺	Tries hard	
☺	Willing to try out new things	
☺	Good at concentrating	
☺	Fun to be with	
☺	Shows concern for others	
☺	Tends not to moan	
☺	Would not easily be persuaded to do something dangerous by friends	

		marks out of 10
✓	Honest	
✓	Tidy	
✓	Cheerful	
✓	Likes to do things well	
✓	Good at giving compliments	
✓	Good at sticking up for self	
✓	A good sense of humour	
✓	Smiles a lot	
✓	Unusual	
✓	Good at fixing things	
✓	Easy-going	
✓	Thinks of others	

		marks out of 10
➔	Easy to get on with	
➔	Interested in things	
➔	Good at forgiving people	
➔	Good at working in a group	
➔	Flexible	
➔	Good at sticking at something	
➔	Good at making people laugh	
➔	Playful	
➔	Confident	
➔	Interesting to listen to	
➔	Appreciative	
➔	Ambitious	

What do you like doing?

To raise their self-awareness, use the chart on the opposite page and ask your child to simply tick (to indicate they like doing this) or cross (to indicate they do not like it) and put a zero for something in-between for the listed activities. It is likely that the activities they tick will relate to the strengths and preferences they identified in the previous exercises.

Knowing your child's strengths and passions will be a great help in thinking about future careers.

Activity	✓/X	Activity	✓/X
Working in a team		Making things	
Working on your own		Being outside	
Using numbers		Playing sport	
Writing		Fixing things	
Doing art		Chatting to people	
Organising and sorting things		Working out how things work	
Using your imagination		Speaking a different language	
Looking after people		Explaining things to other people	
Drawing designs		Cooking	
Performing		Drawing and painting	
Problem solving		Thinking up new ideas	
Going to new places		Using a computer	
Playing music		Discussing issues	
Helping others		Persuading people	
Gardening		Drawing maps	
Being in charge		Following instructions	
Listening to others		Presenting something to a group of people	

Thinking about the future

When you are 11 or 12 it is hard to relate what you do at school with anything you might do in the future. However, secondary school is the time when your child will probably start to realise what they are good at and what their passions are – not just in terms of academic subjects but also individual strengths and interests. They will discover this from time in lessons, any school clubs they attend and other responsibilities they might take on.

Many of us had little or no idea about what exactly we might do when we left school. This may or may not be true of your child. However, having some kind of vision about what they want in the future can motivate your child to keep trying hard and doing well at school. Also when a young person can link what they do at school directly to a possible future career (or just to broadening their opportunities), it can provide motivation for school work.

In light of the personality, strengths and interests your child has identified in the previous activities, you can now talk about any ambitions they might have for their future. Use the following questions as a prompt.

Which of the following do you think will be important in any job you end up doing?

- You work with people

- You travel around

- You get paid lots of money

- The job changes and you get to do lots of different things

- You get to use your own ideas in your work

- You work with your hands

- You don't just sit in an office

- You work outside

- You get to be your own boss

- You don't have to think too hard

- You gain expert knowledge in something

- Anything else?

Make a list any jobs you think you might like to do in the future.

Which subjects do you think you will need to do well in to do the jobs that interest you?

What and when

Which of the following things do you think you will do and when do you think you will do them?

■ Learn to drive

■ Have children

■ Find a partner that you spend the rest of your life with

■ Leave education

■ Move away from home.

Other ambitions or things you hope to achieve

For example:

♦ meeting someone famous

♦ riding in a hot air balloon

♦ climbing Mount Kilimanjaro

♦ go travelling

♦ skiing

♦ learning a foreign language

♦ learning to play a musical instrument

♦ delivering a performance

♦ writing a book

♦ anything else?

Dealing with homework

Some children struggle with homework. What's more it can cause the child's whole family a lot of distress as the weekly or even nightly 'homework problem monster' raises its ugly head. If you carry on tackling this issue in the same way as you have always done, you are very likely to continue with the same difficulties. Sometimes stepping out of the situation and exploring it with a different perspective can help.

If homework has become a regular problem, try the following steps:

1 Sit down with your child and acknowledge that homework has become a very uncomfortable/distressing/irritating/terrible/not-so-good problem and that things definitely need to change for the better.

2 Work out the details of the problem. What is it exactly that your child is finding difficult? Ask them to place a mark on each spectrum on the table opposite to illustrate what they think about each statement.

3 Take the main problems and work out some solutions to turn into homework rules! Start the thinking by asking, 'When you do your homework well without any problems, what makes that happen?'

4 After a week or so, review the situation. If things have improved your child could be rewarded (e.g. choose what the family is going to have for dinner, choose an activity they want to do and so on). If things have not improved, ask your child what happened and give them a chance to try again.

5 If it seems that the homework situation is never going to improve speak to your child's form tutor and see if together some solutions can be found.

Examples of rules you might develop:

★ No television/computer/games console until all homework is done.

★ I (the parent/carer) promise to glance over each piece of homework once it is completed.

★ Always sit in a quiet room at the desk to do your homework.

★ Mark out on a weekly chart when you are going to complete each piece of homework.

★ There will be no nagging about homework as long as you demonstrate that you can be trusted to complete it.

★ I will tell my teacher when I find homework too easy/hard and I will try to be as specific as I can about what I am finding difficult or what I don't understand.

★ I will always make sure I write clear instructions in my homework diary about the tasks I need to do.

★ I will make a note on a weekly chart to indicate when homework needs to be handed in and always get my homework in on time.

Statement about homework	How much of a problem is this?		
	Giant problem *I feel this is really true* ←	*This might sometimes be a problem* →	**Not a problem at all** *I feel this is not an issue*
I struggle to get my homework in on time			
I often find it too difficult			
I often find it too easy			
I find it hard to settle down to it			
I don't take pride in what I do and am happy just to get it out of the way			
I ask for too much help to complete it			
It takes too much time			
I often get upset or angry about doing it			
I often forget what the tasks actually are			
I often get low marks and this makes me feel bad about homework			
I get in a muddle about which homework needs to be completed by when			
I get distracted by other things when I am doing my homework			
I don't feel anyone takes any interest in my homework			
I don't think homework is important			
I don't feel trusted to just get on with it myself			
I get too much homework some nights and not much on others and I find this hard to manage			

Motivation

Motivation can be something many adults struggle with! The following will help you develop a basic understanding of motivation and give some handy tips to help you develop it in your child.

Motivation is developed when someone can:

✓ set a goal

✓ break the goal down into small steps

✓ be determined in moving towards the goal (using strategies that work for them)

✓ know when they have achieved their goal and explore how effectively they have achieved it.

External motivation can encourage us to do (or not do) something but developing intrinsic and internal motivation means we will self-motivate and will not need others to persuade us to get on and do something.

Info point

There are three different types of motivation:

- **External motivation** – where we do something because we will receive some kind of reward for doing it or it prevents a bad outcome (e.g. a punishment, fine etc).

- **Intrinsic motivation** – where we are motivated by the activity itself because it is enjoyable or interesting.

- **Internal motivation** – where we do something because we value what is produced.

As a parent/carer you may believe that a healthy aim is to help your child become self-motivated. How you encourage them to engage in work is key. You can:

- demonstrate a personal enjoyment in learning

- show an interest in any information about school work that your child shares with you

- praise your child for having a go

- encourage your child to work independently

- focus on what has been learned or what has improved rather than what has been produced (or what final grades were achieved)

- never make comparisons with other children's capabilities or the work they produce

- see making mistakes as a valuable part of learning

- help your child see that everyone can fail at some point and having another go at something you know you find difficult is more praiseworthy than just giving up.

...ying motivated can sometimes be the ...ost difficult part of achieving a goal. When a task seems particularly boring, repetitive or simply beyond us it can be easy to give up or become distracted. Help your child to develop ways to persist with a task and be determined to complete it. Together consider a task that you or your child finds difficult to complete but that they do usually manage to complete (for example tidying up, doing a piece of homework). Next consider what they do to remain motivated. Strategies might include:

♦ imagining how good you will feel once the task is complete

♦ promising yourself some kind of reward for completing the task

♦ setting yourself the challenge of completing the task in a certain amount of time

♦ allowing yourself a break at a particular time or after a particular amount of the task has been completed

♦ splitting the task into different sessions with a clear idea of what will be achieved in each session

♦ asking for help (e.g. talking the task through with someone else to clarify what you need to do or asking someone to check up on you occasionally)

♦ creating a tick list of the different stages of a task, ticking them once done and reflecting upon what you have achieved every now and then.

When you have discussed some different strategies, ask your child how they could be used to approach homework tasks and if they think they might be helpful. Write these strategies on a 'motivation poster' and position on a wall where your child does their homework.

Making mistakes

Achievement in school is often assessed by what your child actually produces rather than how well they get on with the task or how they have 'moved on' from where they started. Their work will often receive the judgement of a tick, a cross or a grade as the outcome. They cannot, therefore, help but compare their work with others or feel bad about a page of crosses, for example. Help your child to understand that everyone makes mistakes, that there is always something to learn from making mistakes and that there is no shame in getting things wrong – especially if you are determined to get it right next time. Fear of failure can sometimes prevent people from even having a go in the first place.

For this reason it is more encouraging to praise the process of your child getting on with their work ('Well done for having a go'/'Great to see you're getting on with your homework') than focusing entirely on what they produce.

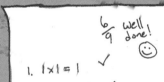

$\frac{6}{9}$ well done! ☺

1. $1 \times 1 = 1$ ✓
2. $3 \times 4 = 12$ ✓
3. $6 \times 8 = 35$ ✗
4. $2 \times 2 = 4$ ✓
5. $3 \times 12 = 100$ ✗
6. $4 \times 6 = 20$ ✓
7. $8 \times 1 = 8$ ✓
8. $100 \times 100 = 200$ ✗
9. $7 \times 3 = 21$ ✓

The problem of bullying

Unless it has been addressed effectively, most children's perception of secondary school is that there is a lot more bullying than there was at primary school. This perception probably comes from myths, media exaggerations (including children's TV programmes), the fact that reports of extreme behaviours stick in our memories and the image that kids just get tougher as they get older!

Of course bullying certainly does happen but it's not as common as people might be lead to believe. The role most children are likely to find themselves in – is not of bullying or being bullied – but that of being a witness to bullying.

When bullying does happen, however, it is a very serious problem and should never be ignored. Bullying can knock a child's self-worth and confidence, can cause extreme stress, illness or depression, have a negative effect on academic achievement, make children reluctant to attend school and in the most extreme cases can result in a child or young person taking their life. It is important, therefore that you spend some time making your child aware of some of the main issues about bullying – especially if your child's school doesn't focus much on this.

Some schools tackle the issue of bullying extremely effectively. These schools:

- Fully acknowledge the potentially devastating effects of bullying.

- Make sure the whole school community (including parents/carers) knows what bullying is, the procedures for reporting it and how it is dealt with (they have a clear and effective anti-bullying policy).

- Have consistent anti-bullying messages and staff who demonstrate anti-bullying behaviours.

- Understand the scope of the different ways a person can be bullied.

- Look out for signs of bullying.

- Have a culture of reporting bullying and encouraging pupils to tell.

- Have a clear procedure for reporting and dealing with bullying, including check-ups shortly after and some months later that confirm the bullying has stopped.

- Monitor bullying incidents and how safe pupils report they feel in school.

- Re-visit the issue annually (often during national anti-bullying week) to remind everyone of its seriousness and how it is dealt with.

 Info point

What is bullying?

For behaviour to be described as bullying it:

- is deliberate

- is usually repeated over a period of time

- causes physical or emotional hurt.

With bullying, there is always an imbalance of power and the target of the bullying usually feels they cannot stick up for themselves.

Raising awareness of what bullying is goes part way towards tackling it.

What do you know about bullying?

You can use the quiz opposite to test your own and your child's knowledge of bullying. *Answers can be found on page 76.*

Signs to look out for if you think your child is being bullied

They:

☹ want to stay home and feign illness frequently

☹ complain of headaches, stomach aches, pains etc

☹ lose interest in school work and participating in things generally – even things they enjoy

☹ have difficulty concentrating and are easily distracted

☹ appear to be lonely and isolated and not have many or any friends

☹ show a change in their eating habits – particularly a loss of appetite

☹ appear to have lost confidence

☹ are nervous, worried, insecure, overly sensitive, quick to avoid talking to you, cautious, irritable, aggressive, and/or clingy

☹ have scratches, bruises

☹ find personal belongings go missing without an obvious explanation.

		TRUE or FALSE
1.	If someone calls someone a nasty name once, it is definitely bullying.	
2.	If a person continuously feels like they cannot stick up for themselves, they are being bullied.	
3.	Some people deserve to be bullied.	
4.	The bully is always bigger than the person they bully.	
5.	Bullying can make people very miserable, become ill and really dread coming to school.	
6.	Some bullies make people hand over their possessions.	
7.	Bullying always involves hitting someone.	
8.	The law says that schools have to know what they are going to do if bullying happens.	
9.	If you see someone being bullied the best thing to do is ignore it.	
10.	Bullying should always be reported. If bullying does not stop, it needs to be reported again.	
11.	Some people do not report that they are being bullied.	
12.	Bullying usually means that a person has been nasty to you more than once.	
13.	If you are bullied, you need to tell someone and keep telling people until someone makes the bullying stop.	
14.	Some bullies use mobile phones and/or the internet to bully. It 's not a good idea to give your mobile phone number or email address out to everyone.	
15.	Deliberately ignoring someone and leaving them out can be bullying.	
16.	Only boys bully.	
17.	Bullying needs to be taken seriously.	
18.	If you see someone being bullied you should always step in and help the person being bullied.	
19.	People that bully others need help.	
20.	Children and young people can ring ChildLine (0800 1111) for advice about what to do if they are being bullied at any time of the day or night and the calls are free.	

What to do if you think your child might be being bullied

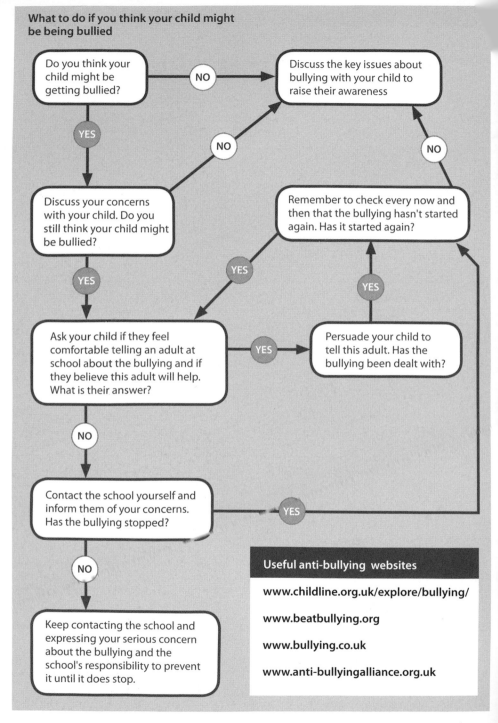

Do you think your child might be getting bullied? — **NO** → Discuss the key issues about bullying with your child to raise their awareness

YES ↓

Discuss your concerns with your child. Do you still think your child might be bullied? — **NO** → Discuss the key issues about bullying with your child to raise their awareness

YES ↓

Ask your child if they feel comfortable telling an adult at school about the bullying and if they believe this adult will help. What is their answer? — **YES** → Persuade your child to tell this adult. Has the bullying been dealt with?

NO ↓

Remember to check every now and then that the bullying hasn't started again. Has it started again? — **NO** → Discuss the key issues about bullying with your child to raise their awareness

YES (Persuade your child...) ↑ → Remember to check every now and then that the bullying hasn't started again.

YES (Remember to check...) → Ask your child if they feel comfortable...

Contact the school yourself and inform them of your concerns. Has the bullying stopped? — **YES** → Remember to check every now and then that the bullying hasn't started again.

NO ↓

Keep contacting the school and expressing your serious concern about the bullying and the school's responsibility to prevent it until it does stop.

Useful anti-bullying websites

www.childline.org.uk/explore/bullying/

www.beatbullying.org

www.bullying.co.uk

www.anti-bullyingalliance.org.uk

E-safety

As your child progresses through secondary school they are likely to use a computer independently for increasing amounts of time, both for research and social networking. It's important that they are made aware of safety measures that need to be taken when using the internet and other technology such as mobile phones.

A very good website outlining age appropriate e-safety to children and young people is provided by the Child Exploitation and Online Protection Centre (CEOP). It includes information about how to report offensive or illegal sites: **www.thinkuknow.co.uk**

Some basic safety measures include:

1 Only give your e-mail address and mobile number to friends you completely trust.

2 Never pass on someone else's e-mail address or phone number without their permission.

3 Always keep your mobile phone with you.

4 Don't use your real name on social networking sites.

5 Never post personal details anywhere online such as your address, school, telephone number or details about yourself or your family.

6 Don't tell anyone your passwords.

7 Never reply to nasty messages – save them and go and tell an adult.

8 Think twice before posting anything (e.g. photos and videos) onto social networking sites or sending photos by phone of yourself or anyone else – remember once they are out there anyone can see them.

9 Never feel pressurised into putting something onto a social networking site or sending it by phone.

10 Never arrange to meet someone you don't know through the internet or by mobile phone. There are some people out there that use the internet to meet children to cause them harm. These people might pretend to be your age and use false photographs.

11 If you accidentally stumble across websites that contain images that upset you, block that site.

12 If someone makes you very uncomfortable by what they are saying to you on a social networking site e.g. they are making sexual comments, block them and make a report to the CEOP: www.thinkuknow.co.uk

13 If you stumble across racist material or images of child sexual abuse – these are illegal and need to be reported to the Internet Watch Foundation: **www.iwf.org.uk**

14 If someone does use technology to bully you, tell a trusted adult. Mobile phone companies have become efficient in tracing nasty phone calls and texts. Many social networking sites also have a way that you can report nasty messages. You can get sound advice from **Childline, tel: 0800 1111** which is a free and confidential helpline for children. Their website also gives help and advice **www.childline.org.uk**

What do you know about bullying? *(Answers)*

1. If someone calls someone a nasty name once, it is definitely bullying.

   FALSE – *a one-off incident is only bullying if the person felt they really could not defend themselves and they were scared that it might reoccur.*

2. If a person continuously feels like they cannot stick up for themselves, they are being bullied.

   TRUE

3. Some people deserve to be bullied.

   FALSE – *but sometimes people who have been bullied blame themselves and this makes them less likely to tell an adult what is happening.*

4. The bully is always bigger than the person they bully.

   FALSE – *it has nothing to do with size. There is always a power imbalance when bullying happens.*

5. Bullying can make people very miserable, become ill and really dread coming to school.

   TRUE

6. Some bullies make people hand over their possessions.

   TRUE

7. Bullying always involves hitting someone.

   FALSE – *there are many different ways in which a person can be bullied, for example: being teased, having nasty text messages sent to or about them, having embarrassing photos or photos with nasty labels posted up on social networking sites, having possessions stolen or damaged etc*

8. The law says that schools have to know what they are going to do if bullying happens.

   TRUE – *by law a school must have an anti-bullying policy or clear guidance about how to deal with bullying in another policy (e.g. behaviour policy)*

9. If you see someone being bullied the best thing to do is ignore it.

   FALSE – *to combat bullying everyone needs to feel that it is their responsibility to do something about it. There should be a way of telling a member of staff about any bullying you might have witnessed.*

10. Bullying should always be reported. If bullying does not stop, it needs to be reported again.

    TRUE – *everyone has the right to be free from bullying.*

11. Some people do not report that they are being bullied.

    TRUE – *sometimes the bully might be forcing them not to tell; they might think they should be able to stop the bullying themselves; they might not know who to tell; they might be scared of being bullied more if they tell an adult; they might be scared that the adult won't believe them or do anything to help; they might feel ashamed and embarrassed about being bullied etc.*

12. Bullying usually means that a person has been nasty to you more than once.

    TRUE – *bullying happens repeatedly over a period of time.*

13. If you are bullied, you need to tell someone and keep telling people until someone makes the bullying stop.

    TRUE – *it is crucial that you find someone who makes the bullying stop so if the first person you tell does nothing to help, find someone else to tell.*

14. Some bullies use mobile phones and/or the internet to bully. It's not a good idea to give your mobile phone number or email address out to everyone.

    TRUE

15. Deliberately ignoring someone and leaving them out can be bullying.

    TRUE

16. Only boys bully.

    FALSE

17. Bullying needs to be taken seriously.

    TRUE

18. If you see someone being bullied you should always step in and help the person being bullied.

    FALSE – *you should never put yourself deliberately in danger. If the bullying is becoming very dangerous the best thing to do would be to get an adult to the scene very quickly.*

19. People that bully others need help.

    TRUE – *people bully for a number of bad reasons. They need help to learn new positive behaviours if they are going to be happy in life.*

20. Children and young people can ring ChildLine **(0800 1111)** for advice about what to do if they are being bullied at any time of the day or night and the calls are free.

    TRUE

Heading for the teenage years

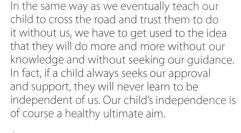

You will no doubt be seeing evidence of your son or daughter growing up as they reach secondary school age. Approaching adolescence in itself is a very transitional time! It's the time when your child no longer wants to be considered a child but is some way from being fully an adult. Negotiating a balance between the freedoms your child feels they are entitled to and how much you feel is safe (or that you are prepared to give them) can be a minefield! However, your child will one day be completely independent of you so the process of their becoming more self-reliant must start somewhere.

Your child is changing and therefore it does seem inevitable that your parenting style will need to adapt. Your parenting will no longer be solely about controlling – not if you want to preserve your relationship with them into adulthood and watch them grow into well-rounded, independent and confident individuals!

Protect or equip?

As a parent, we often feel the need to protect our children. When they are small, they need us to protect them because they cannot learn the skills to protect themselves. For this reason we would never let a two year old cross the road by themselves. However, as our children grow up, we need to steadily move away from protecting them towards equipping them to protect themselves.

In the same way as we eventually teach our child to cross the road and trust them to do it without us, we have to get used to the idea that they will do more and more without our knowledge and without seeking our guidance. In fact, if a child always seeks our approval and support, they will never learn to be independent of us. Our child's independence is of course a healthy ultimate aim.

To some extent, by the time your child goes to secondary school, you have done most of your influential parenting. It's time to start trusting that you have laid the solid foundations that will mean your child can confidently make informed choices and learn from any mistakes they make.

DANGER
AHEAD

How to communicate with your child

When your child was younger, you might have been quite directive and told them exactly what to do and what not to do. As your child grows up, this approach is likely to work less well.

As your child grows older communication needs to become more and more collaborative and you will need to work with your child to agree a way forward over any issue. Problems, conflicts of interest, differences of opinions and disagreements are bound to occur between you. However, a shift away from the parent/carer automatically being right and the child always having to accept what the parent says needs to happen – if you are to allow them to develop independent thinking, self-reliance and to grow up. If we always took an authoritarian approach with the other adults in our lives we would not get very far!

Go and wash the dishes NOW!

When talking to your adolescent or pre-teen child:

1 Try to always be respectful towards them.

2 Try not to react to something you don't like the sound of with an automatic and shocked 'no'. Listen to what it is that your child is attracted to, acknowledge their wishes and explore it together. Ask your child to explain their wishes in detail and ask them to explain more about what they want, why they want it and what is involved. The chances are, that when their 'wish' has been really explored and researched (including risks, regrets people might have had, reasons why people do something etc), they might well change their mind anyway.

3 Walk away if your child becomes defiant, rude or dismissive towards you. Don't be tempted to mirror their mood as you will be replicating and therefore role-modelling the very behaviour that wound you up in the first place!

4 Try not to talk when one or both of you are upset or angry. Take time out and return to the topic later when you are in a better frame of mind.

5 Be aware that their adolescent sensitivity will make your child respond particularly badly to comments you make to remind them to do something. If you say, 'Have you washed your face?' they might hear, 'I don't trust you to look after yourself'. You might see what you are saying as a gentle reminder, they will see it as nagging. It's important to show your child that you trust them to do what needs doing. Instead of 'Have you done your homework?' you might like to try, 'I know you're very good at organising yourself but I need some peace of mind and need to ask if you have done your homework'.

6 Always be clear about what needs to happen to remedy a bad situation e.g. 'I need you to earn back my trust by...'.

7 Be prepared to say sorry if you lose your temper (and blame your loss of temper if you later go back on what you said you would do when you were angry!).

8 Be prepared to listen. Never underestimate the power of listening. When your child has a problem, they know more about the problem than you do simply because it is their problem. They, therefore, have the understanding of the problem that is needed to find a suitable solution. People often find their own solutions by talking something through to someone who is mostly just listening.

9 Remain solution focused. Ask yourself what is the best outcome in any situation and how can you get there together? (Or consider when things have worked well and what contributed to making it work well.)

But that's so unfair!

10 Try to acknowledge the full spectrum of options when discussing anything. It is better to acknowledge that people engage in risk-taking behaviours (e.g. smoke, take drugs) and discuss why they might do so than to pretend these behaviours don't exist in an attempt to protect your child. It is better to equip your child with information than to ignore an issue.

11 Always link increased rights with increased responsibility. This is a cliché but it's useful to join the two in discussions with your child over greater freedoms. With each extra 'right' your child is given, explain their responsibilities towards the newly acquired 'right' (see table below).

'Right'	'Responsibility'
Go to a town/city with a friend	Be mindful of safety, return at the agreed time and keep me (the parent/carer) informed of your whereabouts
Go to a party	Be trusted to behave responsibily
Get your ears pierced	Keep them clean and follow school rules about earirngs

A helpful view of adolescence

You might be able to remember your own experience of adolescence...

- hormones take you on an emotional rollercoaster

- a growth spurt means you wake up with your hands in a different position each day which makes you prone to clumsiness

- your body grows lots of bits it didn't used to have

- you are ridiculously self-consciousness

- significant physiological changes in your brain wiring cause a general disorientation

- you have a need to broaden your horizons and sponge up new interests and attitudes that might clash with your family

- you have an awakening sexual attraction to others

- you want to test boundaries

- you have an ever-shifting identity.

Is it any wonder then that this makes adolescence a very, very tricky time! From the outside it can, quite frankly on occasions, appear ugly. But however testing it gets for you, it pays to remember that, inside your child is full of tumultuous sensitivity and can be finding life extremely difficult. They are tender on the inside but they simply cannot help what they dish out sometimes. They need your unconditional love and positive regard more than ever!

It is also useful to remember that they will eventually come out of the other end. All you can hope for in this time is that you have preserved a healthy relationship with your child so you can reap the benefits of what emerges from the other end.

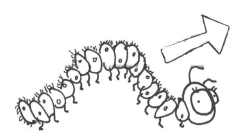

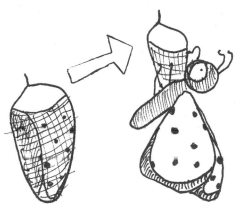

Employ some empathy!

With the above description of adolescence in mind it is a miracle that the vast majority of us emerge intact! Imagine how easily we give tolerance and forgiveness to those struggling because they are enduring an obviously traumatic event in their lives. Well it's good to remember there is a lot going on during adolescence and therefore a little empathy and forgiveness for mishaps is probably needed! Instead of, 'She just cannot remember to take her PE kit to school when she needs it' think, 'She is really struggling with that. What could I do to help?'

Puberty

At around the same time as a child transfers to secondary school, most children embark upon puberty. Puberty brings a lot of change in a relatively short space of time.

If your child is willing to talk about the changes of puberty with you, you might like to discuss the following.

- The details about the actual physical changes of puberty (see pages 82-83 as a starting point).

- The practicalities of dealing with spots, periods, wet dreams and shaving.

- The emotional aspects of the changes of puberty.

- The names for external sexual organs.

- That puberty can start anywhere between the ages of eight and fourteen. People can feel awkward about being the first or the last to start puberty.

- No one should ever make personal comments about the changes someone is experiencing.

- Puberty can be a time when you feel self-conscious but you can be reassured that you are probably the only person who has noticed whatever it is that is making you feel this way.

- It is inappropriate to make fun of any changes that happen during puberty.

- Many young people wonder if they are 'normal' during puberty. This can be part of adapting to a changing body.

- The hormones rushing around the body during puberty can make a person feel really happy one minute and grumpy or tearful the next. The hormones do eventually settle down.

- During puberty, young people often start to fancy other people. This can be something that can cause distress, worry or very intense feelings. It's a good idea to talk concerns through with a trusted friend or adult.

- What masturbation is and that it does not harm you.

- You need to start to pay more attention to personal hygiene at the onset of puberty.

If your child is not comfortable discussing these topics with you there are many great books that cover all your child might need to know. Your child could read such a book privately if they prefer.

Info point

When do the changes of puberty happen?

The changes of puberty happen to all girls and boys but they can start at different times. Generally, they start later in boys than in girls. In some people they start before the age of ten but in others it can be as late as fourteen. The changes can also take place at a different rate. For some people all the changes of puberty can take just two years and in others it can take as long as four years.

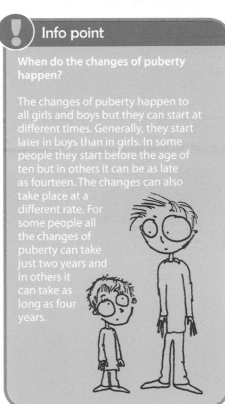

81

Girls

Most girls start puberty between the ages of nine and thirteen. For girls, puberty usually starts with breast growth. A girl might notice small tender lumps under the nipple that grow bigger over the next few years. As breasts develop, a girl may choose to wear a bra.

Around the same time, soft hair starts to grow around the pubic area (the area between the legs) and under the arms. This hair eventually becomes thick and curly. A girl's body shape will gradually change: her hips become wider, her waist thinner and some fat tends to build up on the stomach, buttocks and legs. This gives the girl the more curvy shape of a woman.

A girl's periods tends to happen towards the end of puberty, somewhere between nine and sixteen years of age. Most girls start their periods between one and a half and two years after their breasts first start to develop, however, it can be after as short as six months or as long as three years. A few months before the start of a girl's first period, she will notice a white mucus discharge coming from her vagina.

Boys

Most boys start puberty between the ages of ten and fourteen. For boys, puberty often starts with a growth spurt. A boy's muscles will grow and he will get taller and develop broader shoulders.

At some point after the start of puberty a boy's voice will get deeper. It can happen as young as 11 or as old as 17. A boy will first notice that his voice sounds like it's cracking and it will go deep at times and squeaky at others. This whole process can take from a couple of months to a year.

Hair will appear under a boy's arms, on his legs and face and above his penis. Hair might grow on a boy's chest during puberty, or later, or not at all.

During puberty a boy's penis and testicles grow larger and he may have more erections than he had in childhood. Also during puberty, a boy will start to ejaculate. This means that he produces semen which comes out from the end of his penis. This can happen as early as the age of 12, or as late as 16. At the beginning, the semen might be quite clear, but by the end of puberty, it is bright white.

A positive self-image

Puberty can be a time when a child feels incredibly self-conscious and often wonders if they are 'normal'. This is partly due to the physical changes they are experiencing but also down to rampaging hormones making life a little uncomfortable. Also the messages children and young people receive from the media – particularly plentiful images of beautiful models and actors – can often leave them feeling physically inadequate and with a very narrow idea of what is considered attractive.

The media and peer influence are both powerful forces to be reckoned with and if your child has a poor self-image it is unlikely to improve overnight.

You can help improve your child's self-image over time by:

☺ regularly making reference to the fact that a person's personality and achievements are more important than what they look like.

☺ regularly complimenting them on their qualities e.g. helpful, considerate to others, optimistic, sporty, determined etc.

☺ discussing how there are behaviours that can make a person more and less attractive (e.g. friendliness/scowling). In other words, attractiveness does not depend solely on what nature gave us.

☺ helping your child to receive compliments from others. Teach them to say 'thank you' when someone says something nice about them.

☺ encouraging your child to give compliments to others (which will in turn mean they receive more compliments).

☺ celebrating the fact that we are all different and that the world would be really dull if we were all the same.

And with respect to actual physical appearance:

- Remind your child that the models shown in adverts are airbrushed and wearing a lot of carefully applied make-up. They wouldn't look so perfect if you met them in real life.

- Help your child understand that even people who look naturally beautiful often still have doubts about how they look. Anyone can choose to focus on the bits they don't like about their appearance. Alternatively, you could focus on the bits you like about yourself. There is no such thing as a perfect person!

- Discuss how the images in magazines might make people feel about themselves.

- Discuss which behaviours you can adopt to make yourself more attractive e.g. smile, be kind, listen to others, make people laugh etc.

- Tell your child that research has shown that everyone becomes more attractive to others the more familiar they become.

- Never compare your child's appearance with another child's appearance.

- Teach your child to reframe any nasty comment they receive. For example, remember that a nasty comment usually says more about the person that says it than the person they're saying it to.

Sexual attraction

As your child grows up they are likely to become sexually attracted to others. Quite often, because of the novelty of this there is a temptation for some adults to tease, or worse, belittle their child's experience of falling for another person or having a crush on a celebrity! However, if these adults are reminded of the intensity with which they experienced crushes on others in their teenage years, they soon realise how inappropriate teasing is.

Your child might also experience the pain of being rejected by another. Your perspective on life might well have taught you that they will get over this experience in a relatively short time but at the time their pain is real and extremely intense. It is best to take it seriously and give them sincere support.

Put risks into perspective

If aliens were sent tabloid newspapers to acquaint themselves with what happens on Earth they would get a much distorted view of the planet. They would have an exaggerated view of the prevalence of knife crime, teenage pregnancy, drug taking, binge drinking and so on. Rarely does the media report a story of the vast majority of children and young people out there behaving incredibly responsibly. Our teenagers are much maligned by the tabloid press in the UK and sadly many people believe what they say – including teenagers themselves.

This exaggerated view of what is happening 'out there' can be very unhelpful as it starts to make people believe that these extreme behaviours are more 'normal' and common than they actually are. So when it comes to risk-taking behaviours, the first thing to remember is they are almost definitely less widespread than you probably think. You need to be aware of this and so does your child.

Risk-taking behaviours – how to approach them

When some children hit the teenage years they can be more likely to test boundaries; boundaries that previously prevented them from encountering potential dangers. This is not true of all children but the following can help you think about how you broach risk-taking behaviours with your child.

In fact, research has shown that giving children and young people the true statistics about risk-taking behaviours (e.g. drug taking, smoking, binge drinking, early sex etc) has more impact on reducing these behaviours (as they realise that not many of their peers are actually engaging in them) than simply telling them not to do these things.

"Every teenager is doing something really risky nearly all the time"

Consider how you discuss things

Think back to your teenage years. If you were told not to do something, was that always effective? If you were told never to drink alcohol ever in your life, do you think that would have worked? Your child sees people smoke, they see people drink alcohol (and enjoy themselves) and engage in other behaviours that you might not prefer for your child. It's better to acknowledge and explore these choices people make than to just tell your child not to do them or never mention them in an attempt to pretend they never happen.

It is a good idea to discuss all behaviours in terms of choices a person might make and explore reasons why they might make them (peer influence, rebellion, lack of self-respect, a nice sensation etc). This can help your child apply some consideration to any decisions they make and with this information, hopefully their decision will be well informed.

Also be wary of using shock tactics. If, for example, you told your child that everyone who drinks behaves in a dangerous way that puts their safety at risk, the first time they drink and behave responsibly they will dismiss what you have said. It is important to be realistic about what happens when people make different choices.

Challenge media messages

Some of the messages children receive from the media (and other sources) are not accurate or realistic and in the absence of adults to help them process this information, they can be left confused, with 'unhealthy' ideas or exaggerated views. The media, for example, can lead children to believe:

- all teenagers binge drink a lot

- bullying happens all the time

- sex is always exciting, fun, easy and uncomplicated

- most people have sex before they are 16

- what you look like is the most important thing about you and there are very narrow ideas about what is considered attractive

- to be a successful man, you have to have sex with lots of women

- to be a successful woman, you must look sexy

- knife crime happens all the time.

Spending time with your child to help them understand the media and how it can give us distorted views of the world is time well spent. Help your child:

- understand the purpose of advertising (to get you to buy things so they use eye-catching images of people and can exaggerate some information about the product)

- explore the methods advertisers use to sell products (and how persuasive they can be)

- challenge the message that the way people look and behave on adverts and in films is 'normal'

- understand what makes something newsworthy and the impression these stories can give us about the world (shocking, extreme, unusual, rare so it stands out)

- understand that the media can give us exaggerated views of the frequency (and therefore likelihood) of tragic or shocking events

- understand that soap operas give a distorted view of everyday life or they would be dull to watch!

What am I going to do? My hair is so dull!

Sit with your child and explore their attitudes to the following topics. Challenge any views that you feel are unrealistic:

→ alcohol
→ drugs
→ teenage pregnancy
→ abortion
→ sex
→ crime
→ bullying
→ what men have to be like
→ what women have to be like
→ pornography
→ violence
→ child abduction
→ what is expected of you if you are in a relationship with someone.

bullying

alcohol

violence

teen pregnancy

crime

Give your child information

Information does not harm or scare children and young people if it's given in a sensitive way with opportunities for them to ask questions. When you consider the variety of sources that young people pick up information from (e.g. TV adverts, graffiti, shop displays/posters, the internet, computer games, pop video images, TV programmes, their school friends, older siblings etc) you can see that they can easily end up confused by inaccurate, distorted or 'unhealthy' messages.

Know that your child is likely to be exposed to a wide range of information about a variety of things you might not always feel comfortable about. It's better that you have discussed these things with your child so they have a more accurate and balanced view of the issues than these other sources would leave them with. It's also better that you've discussed these things before they are likely to encounter them. If they are equipped with accurate information about an issue they are less likely to be influenced by other sources and more likely to react in a measured way. Topics you might want to give your child information about include:

→ the physical and emotional changes of puberty

→ alcohol – the effects, why adults drink, what 'drinking in moderation' is, when drinking becomes risky (including the dangers of driving under the influence of alcohol or getting in a car when the driver is drunk)

→ smoking – the health effects, reasons why people start smoking, the cost, what to say if you were offered a cigarette and you did not want to smoke

→ drugs – the fact there are a variety of drugs, the effects, why people take drugs, the risks, how to resist drugs

→ the risks of sex – pregnancy, regret, being pressurised into doing things you don't want to, not pressurising others, sexually transmitted infections, abortion, contraception and safer sex

→ what a positive sexual relationship would be like – including trust, communication, safer sex etc

→ media – see 'Challenge media messages' on page 86.

→ bullying – see 'The problem of bullying' on page 70.

→ safety – see 'E-safety on page 73 and 'Keeping safe out and about' on page 91.

→ body image – see 'A positive self-image' on page 84.

There are lots of great books and leaflets that can be used to support these conversations with your child. One source of support for parents/carers with a variety of topics is Parentline Plus

www.parentlineplus.org.uk

tel: 0808 800 2222

Keeping safe out and about

Your child's increasing independence will mean that they are out and about on their own more often than when they were younger. Most schools cover what a child needs to do to stay safe when they are out and about but before your child goes to secondary school is a good time to drop in a few reminders such as:

- Make sure that your mum/dad/carer knows:

  - who you are with

  - where you are going

  - when you will be back

  - if possible, a phone number that you can be reached at.

  Alternatively always have your mobile phone with you and make sure it is charged.

- Never go off with anyone unless it is planned by your mum/dad/carer. This certainly includes getting into a car or going into someone's house without your parent's or carer's permission. (Unfortunately some people harm children. Not many people do, but if they seem to be trying to take you away without telling anyone, then they are probably up to no good.) If a car pulls up close to you to ask directions, keep your distance.

- Always be mindful of road safety – when crossing the road, walking along a path and cycling. Never let your guard down. Be aware that you can be distracted when you are with your friends.

- If you are in a busy place with someone, arrange a meeting place that you can go to in case you get separated.

- Know that 'safe people' who you can ask for help or directions from are a police officer, a shopkeeper, or someone who has a young child.

- Always look confident and purposeful if someone approaches you and you are not sure what their intentions are. Bullies and dangerous adults are more likely to pick on a child or young person who looks unsure of themselves.

How about some 'controlled' excitement?

If your child appears to be a bit of a thrill-seeker or even if they are not, why not provide slightly unusual experiences for them – with you very much in control of their safety? For example, a treasure hunt in a graveyard at night, an independent journey to a large town or city, rock climbing, fairground rides, volunteering in a workplace and so on.

91

Developing emotional literacy

Awareness of emotional literacy and its benefits has increased in recent years. Some of the basic lessons being learnt in some schools through the use of the Social and Emotional Aspects of Learning (SEAL) curriculum can go a long way in helping children to manage their emotions effectively. As the teenage years can be tough on the emotions, some awareness of these basic lessons is extremely helpful to both parents/carers and their children.

! Info point

What is emotional literacy and what are its benefits?

Emotional literacy can be defined as being aware of the emotions you are feeling, knowing what might be causing them, knowing the best way of expressing what you are feeling and being aware of others' emotions and adjusting your behaviour as a result.

Emotional literacy helps us to learn from our experiences, deal with challenges in a more positive way, develop the ability to bounce back from knock-backs, interact with others more effectively, make and keep healthy relationships and reduce stress. It's a good thing and it's never too late to learn.

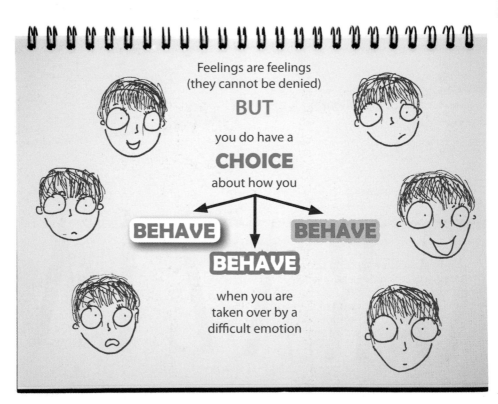

Feelings are feelings
(they cannot be denied)
BUT
you do have a
CHOICE
about how you
BEHAVE   BEHAVE
BEHAVE
when you are
taken over by a
difficult emotion

One key message about emotions that is being taught is that emotions are emotions. It can be quite hard to control how we feel in response to another person's actions or events that happen. We feel what we feel. However, what we can do is choose what we do and how we behave in response to an emotion. For example, you cannot help it if someone else's actions make you angry and anger can be an appropriate response. Anger is part of the human condition and it can sometimes bring about beneficial changes. However when you are angry, it is your choice whether you go and hit the person that caused you to get angry or take time to calm down and talk to the person later about what happened.

For this reason, it is always important to acknowledge your child's right to feel the way they do. Telling someone they have no right to be angry is harmful. If they are angry, they are angry! However, strategies can be taught that mean damaging behaviours – particularly anger – can be avoided. If your child is wired up in a way that means they have quite a short fuse you might like to discuss such strategies. For example:

- **EXERCISE** – run or punch a pillow!

- **RELAXATION** – deep breaths, imagining yourself floating on a cloud, listening to calming music

- **DISTRACTION** – moving to a new place, doing something different, chanting a calming phrase like 'stay calm' over and over, thinking about a time when you felt great, trying to change your mood so you are choosing not to focus on what made you angry.

To help your child become better at managing difficult feelings – anger in particular, you can talk about the following together:

1. Recognise the physical signs that tell you that you are becoming angry e.g. clenching teeth, breathing more quickly, sweating, scowling etc

2. What makes you and your child angry? Explore triggers of anger e.g. someone laughs at you; getting frustrated when you find something difficult.

3. Consider 're-framing' as shown in the table below. A person's action might have made you angry but that might not have been their intention. Reframing can prevent your child from feeling angry.

What happens	What we might think	Reframing
Someone snaps at you when you ask them a question	'She doesn't like me.'	'Oh she is not in a good mood today.'
The ball is never passed to you in a game of football.	'They are deliberately leaving me out.'	'They are all so excited about the game, they are not really thinking about making sure everyone gets the ball at some point.'

4. Teach your child to compose 'I' messages:

- Pinpoint the cause of the uncomfortable feeling and what the feeling is.
- Ask – could anything be done about this cause?
- Create and use an 'I' message.

When you... *explain what they did,*

I felt... *state which emotion,*

I would like you to... *explain what you would like to happen*

e.g. When you laughed at me, I felt embarrassed. I would like you to stop laughing.

'I' messages are good because:

✓ nobody can challenge the statement, 'I felt...'

✓ 'YOU made me angry' is more confrontational and stops the angry person speaking from acknowledging their emotion needs sorting out.

Different ways anger can be expressed

Aggressively – usually makes situations escalate. This is seen as more socially acceptable in males. Probably very appropriate in life or death situations!

Passively – no external response, anger turns inward as self-hatred (e.g. common in self-harmers). More commonly a female response.

Indirectly – complaining about whatever induced the anger. Because the 'moaning' never actually addresses the situation, it is perpetuated and often the person moaning starts to feel more and more negative. This a more typically female response to anger.

Assertively – Does not always work but has much more chance of addressing whatever induced the anger without causing the situation to escalate. ('I' messages.)

Helping your child understand what it's like for you!

Sometimes our children forget we are people with feelings as well! We can appear to endlessly receive and cope with all their tests and tribulations without the impact they have on us having any relevance as far as they are concerned! Making reference to your own experiences (and feelings about your experiences) when you were a teenager can help remind your child that things can have an effect on you.

Likewise, be honest about how you might struggle at times with adapting to a child who is growing up, becoming more independent and has a developing and changing outlook. Explain exactly what you are finding difficult and use it as an excuse for the things you don't always get right! Help your child see that you are also coping with change.

Hopes and dreams for your child

This time of transition is just a fraction of your child's lifetime. As a parent/carer it is easy to become lost in the day-to-day details of everyday living and 'big picture' parenting is hard to get round to! However, if you were to sit down and ask yourself, 'How would I want my child to have developed so that they make the most of life?', what would your list include?

Try the following ideas as a starting point:

✓ Have well-developed self-esteem, self-awareness and self-respect.

✓ Know their own strengths and how to apply them and have future aspirations. Have a good inclination of what their 'passion' is in life and what will make them fulfilled.

✓ Have motivation and a passion for learning and achieving.

✓ Be creative – in their approaches to problem solving in particular. Move away from right and wrong and one 'correct' way of doing anything and be comfortable with making and learning from 'mistakes'.

✓ Develop relationship skills and attitudes – communicating effectively, working in a team/individually, taking responsibility for actions, respecting others and celebrating the differences between people.

✓ Be able to resolve conflicts effectively.

✓ Have the ability to take appropriate care over decisions and dilemmas.

✓ Know how to minimise the risk to their safety, keep healthy, manage emotions and develop positive ways of coping.

✓ Have considered attitudes, values and beliefs and developed their own individual moral framework to guide their actions.

✓ Have a feeling of social responsibility and 'connection'.

Good luck on your journey.